a practical g

CHARITY

ACCOUNTING

PREPARING charity SORP accounts

▼ EDITOR • KATE SAYER ▼

DIRECTORY OF SOCIAL CHANGE

Published by
Directory of Social Change
24 Stephenson Way
London NW1 2DP
Tel. 020 7209 5151; Fax 020 7391 4804
e-mail books@dsc.org.uk
www.dsc.org.uk
from whom further copies and a full publications list are available.

ISBN 1 903991 21 8

British Library Cataloguing in Publication Data
A catalogue record for this book is available from the British Library

Cover design by Penny Drinkwater
Designed and typeset by Penny Drinkwater
Printed and bound by Page Bros., Norwich

Other Directory of Social Change departments in London:
Courses and conferences 020 7209 4949
Charity Centre 020 7209 1015
Charityfair 020 7391 4875
Publicity & Web Content 020 7391 4900
Policy & Research 020 7391 4880

Directory of Social Change Northern Office:
Federation House, Hope Street, Liverpool L1 9BW
Courses and conferences 0151 708 0117
Policy & Research 0151 708 0136

CONTENTS

Acknowledgements   4

Foreword   5

Introduction   7

Glossary   9

1 Charity SORP   15

2 Trustees' annual report   30

3 Risk assessment   40

4 Reserves policy   47

5 Investments   57

6 Grantmaking   71

7 Managing restricted funds   80

8 Allocating costs   100

9 Tangible fixed assets   117

10 Related party transactions   134

Appendix   143

Further information   148

Index   152

ACKNOWLEDGEMENTS

It is usual to thank the people who support and encourage you in the whole process of producing a book. This book is different from earlier ones I have written as it really has been a team effort with managers at Sayer Vincent who are the authors of various chapters. I would therefore like to thank the following for their special efforts:

Liz Rosser

Judith Miller

Jonathan Orchard

Angela Blanchard

I am also really grateful to my partner Helen Elliott, who had the onerous duty of reading the whole book to check it for technical accuracy, only to be told after starting the job that we also needed to meet a printing deadline.

Thanks are also due to the charities that have allowed extracts from their annual reports and accounts to be used in the text as examples.

These include The National Association of Victim Support Schemes, Waste Watch, the British Heart Foundation, Barnardo's, The Guide Dogs for the Blind Association, The Diana, Princess of Wales Memorial Fund, the Wellcome Trust, the City Parochial Foundation and Oxfam GB.

My thanks to Alison Baxter and the publishing team at the Directory of Social Change for their support and for making sure that another project really did happen!

FOREWORD

Public concern with 'accountability' and 'transparency' for charities has always been a feature of life – it's just that it seems to grow in importance. The SORP is just one of the tools available to help translate statutory requirements into the end product. 'How-to' guides are a welcome addition, especially with a SORP that recognised in its title, 'Accounting and Reporting by Charities', that responding to accountability was to be expressed clearly through the trustees' annual report as well as through the financial statements.

I am sure that the layperson believes that the preparation and understanding of charity accounts is really no different from any other set of accounts. Little do they know! I came to charity accounting after many years in the private sector and suffered the rude shock that affects most finance managers new to the sector – fund accounting, designations, SORP, the concept of trusts, primary purpose trading and much else. So this new book, written by a team from Sayer Vincent and amply illustrated, is a welcome addition to existing tools.

The Charity Commission has introduced new golden rules for monitoring compliance with the SORP, which deal equally with the trustees' annual report and the financial statements. *A Practical Guide to Charity Accounting* deals extensively with both reporting requirements and, if followed, should help charities deal properly and appropriately with compliance.

It is no coincidence that three recent government reports on the charity and not-for-profit sector have contained substantial recommendations on reporting and accounting. The Strategy Unit, the Public Accounts Committee and the Treasury have commented on the need for SORP compliance, improved reporting on objectives and achievements, and for better and more accurate information. Yet another reason for seeking help from this practical guide to charity accounting!

David Taylor
Charity Commissioner
November 2002

INTRODUCTION

The first book by the Directory of Social Change and Sayer Vincent on charity accounting was issued following the production of the Statement of Recommended Practice 1995. That edition contained many practical examples of how the SORP could be applied to the accounts of charities of different sizes.

Subsequently, a new version of the SORP was issued in October 2000. The Charity Commission produced a companion volume (CC66 SORP 2000 Example Reports and Accounts), which provided full examples of the SORP in practice, to which Sayer Vincent contributed.

The Directory of Social Change and Sayer Vincent have now produced this new book, written to develop further the techniques and methods needed in order to produce a set of charity accounts to comply with the SORP and best practice. It is addressed largely to those who prepare charity accounts and aims to provide them with an approach for each of the major steps in the production of charity accounts. The topics covered reflect the questions that are most frequently asked, and each chapter has been prepared by a manager at Sayer Vincent who has practical experience of preparing accounts following the charity SORP.

At the time of publication, a report produced by the Strategy Unit of the Cabinet Office entitled *Private Action, Public Benefit* is in a period of consultation. Some of the proposals in the report will affect charity auditing and accounting to some degree if they are translated into legal requirements. For example, the report proposes that the threshold for the statutory audit requirement of charities should be raised to gross income of £1 million. However, the changes proposed and likely to be implemented are chiefly concerning legal aspects of charity form and management. It is likely, however, that the SORP will be revised in the future to take account of changes in Financial Reporting Standards and other accounting changes.

Further information is provided for those who wish to examine a particular issue in greater depth. In addition, regular updated information is available on the Sayer Vincent website (www.sayervincent.co.uk).

About the authors

Kate Sayer is a chartered accountant with over 19 years experience of the charity and not-for-profit sector. She is a member of the SORP Committee working with the Charity Commission and Accounting Standards Board to develop appropriate guidelines for the charity sector.

Angela Blanchard is a qualified chartered accountant who has been with Sayer Vincent for two years. She is an audit manager for a portfolio of charity and not-for-profit clients.

Judith Miller qualified with KPMG and then worked abroad for two years, before returning to a manager position with Sayer Vincent four years ago. As well as managing charity audit clients, Judith leads a number of training courses and develops training and support for trustees of charities.

Jonathan Orchard trained as a chartered accountant with Sayer Vincent and is a manager with the firm. After qualifying, he spent six months overseas with Save the Children Fund working with their internal audit team. He leads assignments for overseas development agencies as well as other charity and not-for-profit clients.

Liz Rosser trained as a chartered accountant with Sayer Vincent and is currently working for the Quality Assurance Agency for Higher Education.

Sayer Vincent is a specialist consultancy focusing on IT, audit, tax, governance and financial management issues for charities and not-for-profit organisations.

Sayer Vincent
8 Angel Gate
City Road
London
EC1V 2SJ
020 7841 6360
info@sayervincent.co.uk
www.sayervincent.co.uk

GLOSSARY

Accountant's report

A report by a qualified accountant on the annual accounts confirming that the accounts have been properly prepared. It is instead of an audit and only available to smaller charitable companies with gross income below £250,000. Also known as a compilation report.

Accruals basis

This is a method of accounting that adjusts the receipts and payments for amounts that should have been collected or paid before the end of the accounting period. Accounts prepared on the accruals basis reflect the income due for the period and the costs incurred.

Assets

Assets are the money, goods and property that an organisation possesses, including any legal rights it may have to receive money, goods, services and property from others.

Balance sheet

Sometimes described as a 'snapshot' of an organisation. A summary of the assets and liabilities of an organisation at a particular date to arrive at the net assets. It also describes the funds or reserves of an organisation.

Capital

The capital of a charity is a restricted fund (or funds) that the trustees must retain for the benefit of the charity and not spend. A capital fund is known as an endowment fund.

Capitalisation

When property or equipment is purchased and treated as an asset on the balance sheet, it is said to be capitalised. This means that the cost is not treated as an operating cost and is not charged to the expense accounts.

Charitable expenditure

This comprises all expenditure directly relating to the objects of the charity. It includes grants payable, the direct costs of supporting charitable activities and the costs of managing and administering the charity. It excludes the costs of generating funds.

Compilation report

See Accountant's report.

Cost of generating funds

These are the costs of obtaining funds for the charity's work, such as bidding for grants, advertising, direct mail, staff time and agent's fees. It also includes investment management fees.

Depreciation

An allowance for wear and tear made on long-lasting property and equipment. An amount charged annually as an expense to spread the cost of fixed assets over their useful economic life.

Designated funds

Designated funds are unrestricted funds that have been earmarked for a particular purpose by the trustees.

Endowment

An endowment is a special type of restricted fund that must be retained intact and not spent.

Expendable endowment

This is a type of endowment fund that trustees have the discretion to eventually convert into expendable income.

Financial Reporting Standard

This is a statement of required good practice for all company accounts and all accounts that purport to give a true and fair view. It is obligatory for all published accounts to comply with Financial Reporting Standards. They are issued by a committee of accounting bodies and cover a range of accounting topics, with updated versions issued regularly.

Financial statements

The accounts of an organisation, including the notes to the accounts and any other statements that are required to be included.

Fixed assets

These are assets that continue to be of value to the organisation year after year, and which the trustees hold on a long-term basis and therefore do not intend to dispose of in the short term.

General funds

These are unrestricted funds that have not been earmarked and may be used generally to further the charity's stated objects.

Governing document

This is the document that establishes the charity and has to be passed by the Charity Commission prior to registration of the charity. It sets out the charity's objects and the rules of the organisation. It may be known by several different names: governing instrument; constitution; trust deed; memorandum and articles of association (for a charitable company); Rules (for an Industrial and Provident Society); explanatory document (in Scotland); or founding deed (in Scotland).

Gross income

Generally means all the income of an organisation for the financial year before deductions of any expenses. Specifically defined for the purposes of thresholds under the Charities Act to exclude all capital (endowment) incoming resources, sale of fixed assets and sale of investments.

Impairment

This is the term used to describe a fall in value of an asset. An impairment review may be required for certain tangible fixed assets. This is usually when some major event has occurred that causes you to think that the previous values ascribed to the asset are no longer valid.

Inalienable asset

An inalienable asset is one that may not be sold or disposed of in the normal way. In some cases, the asset may not be sold at all; for others, there may be restrictions or prescribed circumstances when a sale is allowed.

Income and expenditure account

A summary of the income due and expenditure incurred for a financial year, showing the revenue transactions only.

Incoming resources

All resources available to a charity, including incoming capital (endowment), restricted income, gifts in kind and intangible income.

Independent examination

Charities with gross income and total expenditure not exceeding £250,000 may have an independent examination instead of an audit. This is a type of external examination brought in by the Charities Act 1993 that may be undertaken by anyone with some experience of accounting, but who does not have to be a qualified accountant or auditor. Detailed guidance on the independent examination has been issued by the Charity Commission.

Liabilities

Liabilities are the amounts owed by an organisation at the balance sheet date. The cost will have already have been incurred, but the bill not paid.

Management and administration

These are the costs incurred in the management of the charity's assets, organisational administration and statutory requirements.

Material

Accounts have to be materially correct, that is nothing of great significance should be wrong with them. A mistake is material if it would change or influence the way that a reader of the accounts would view the information contained in the accounts. There is no percentage or rule on what is material. By contrast, an immaterial difference means that even if the amount were 100% correct, it would not be altered.

Net book value

The net book value is calculated for tangible fixed assets by taking the original cost or valuation amount and deducting the accumulated depreciation. The net book value is the amount at which tangible fixed assets are stated in the balance sheet.

Net realisable value

The net realisable value is the likely proceeds from a sale of an asset or goods, less the costs of selling them.

Permanent endowment

This is a type of endowment fund where the trustees must retain the fund intact as capital and use the funds to generate income or hold the assets (depending on the terms of the trust). The trustees have no discretion to convert the endowment into expendable income.

Receipts and payments account

A simple form of accounts that summarises the cash transactions of a charity. An option available to smaller charities.

Registered auditor

An accountant or firm of accountants who are registered to undertake company audits and are regulated in their work by one of the accountancy bodies.

Residual value

The value of an asset at the end of its useful economic life is termed its residual value. This should be estimated when the asset is first acquired.

Restricted fund
This is a fund subject to specific trusts within the objects of the charity (for example, by a letter from the donor at the time of the gift, or by the terms of a public appeal). It may be a capital fund, which cannot be spent but must be retained for the benefit of the charity, or it may be an income fund, which must be spent on the specified purpose within a reasonable time.

Scottish charity
A body established in Scotland and recognised as charitable by the Inland Revenue.

SORP
See Statement of Recommended Practice.

Statement of assets and liabilities
A summary required for charities preparing accounts under the receipts and payments basis. Not the same as a balance sheet; non-monetary assets do not have to be valued.

Statement of Financial Activities (SoFA)
New financial statement introduced especially for charities in the SORP. Summarises all incoming resources and application of resources. Replacing the income and expenditure account as a primary financial statement, it goes further by bringing together all the transactions of a charity.

Statement of Recommended Practice (SORP) Guidance on the appropriate treatment of items in the accounts of specialised bodies.

Stock
The value of goods on hand at the balance sheet date will be included in stock under current assets.

Support costs
These are part of the charitable expenditure and may be the management of projects from a central office. They may include a fair proportion of central office running costs.

Tangible fixed assets
Long-term assets that have some on-going use or purpose in the operations of the charity, such as buildings and equipment.

Total expenditure
All the outgoings of an organisation for a financial year, excluding purchases of fixed assets and investments.

Unrestricted funds

These are funds held for the general purposes of the charity, to be spent within the stated objects.

Voluntary income

Donated income and grants are often grouped together as voluntary income. This is funding freely given to a charity without an expectation of a service in return.

1 ▼ Charity SORP

The format of the accounts for all charities is guided by the Statement of Recommended Practice: Accounting and Reporting by Charities (SORP), issued by the Charity Commission in conjunction with the Accounting Standards Board. The Charities Act 1993 provides the legal framework for the audit and accounts of unincorporated charities in England and Wales, together with the Accounting Regulations 1995 and 2000 issued under the act. Charitable companies still refer to Companies Act legislation for determining whether a statutory audit is required, however Charitable companies need to follow the SORP in order for their accounts to give a true and fair view. This will also be the case for Industrial and Provident Societies that have charitable objects. There are special provisions for small charities; these vary depending on whether the charity is a company or not. The detailed requirements for charities of different sizes and legal status are set out in the Appendix. This chapter focuses on the requirements for all medium-sized and large charities, and also for small charities following the SORP.

Charities in Scotland and Northern Ireland do need to follow the SORP as it represents best practice for charity accounting. They do not have to comply with the regulations, however, and there are separate statutory requirements. (*See Further information.*) This book focuses on the SORP and best practice, which will apply to all charities regardless of legal status.

FORM OF CHARITY ACCOUNTS

The Statement of Recommended Practice: Accounting by Charities (SORP) was introduced in October 1995 and a revised version (called Accounting and Reporting by Charities) was issued in October 2000. This version is often referred to as SORP 2000. The revised version applies to accounting periods commencing on or after 1 January 2001. It contains guidance on the suitable treatment and presentation of charity accounts and represents good practice. It incorporates the Financial Reporting Standards (FRS) and provides an interpretation of these for charities where applicable. The SORP applies to all charities, except for a few instances where there is another more specialised SORP in existence, as in the case of higher education institutions and registered social landlords.

The SORP has evolved to deal with particular aspects of charities' activities and operations. The most important of these are dealt with in some detail in other chapters of this book. The basic concepts and underlying principles of the SORP are dealt with here.

Scottish charities have to conform to legislation in Scotland as well as the SORP, and so unincorporated charities are required to produce an income and expenditure account as a primary statement, as well as a Statement of Financial Activities (SoFA). The law on charities in Northern Ireland does not specify the content and format of accounts.

Format and contents of charity financial statements

- Legal and administrative details
- Trustees' report
- Statement of Financial Activities
- Summary of income and expenditure (only required for charitable companies in certain circumstances)
- Balance sheet
- Cashflow statement (where required for larger charities under FRS 1)
- Notes to the accounts.

NO PROFIT

The SORP tries to move away from the concept of profit as the measure of success or failure. The profit concept is not appropriate to charities, as charity law requires them to use all funds to further their charitable objects. In addition, charities are not owned by a proprietor or by shareholders in the same way as commercial entities. There is no overall objective of maximising shareholder value; rather there is an overall objective of maximising the impact of the charity for its beneficiaries, which cannot be so easily measured in financial terms.

The profit and loss account (income and expenditure account) is therefore replaced by a SoFA. This statement brings together all the resources available to the charity and shows how these have been used to fulfil the charity's objectives.

INCOMING RESOURCES

Rather than simply showing *income*, charities have to show all *incoming resources* in the SoFA. The term 'incoming resources' has a wider meaning than income, including gifts in kind, intangible income and new endowments.

Incoming resources should be recognised in the SoFA in the year in which they arise. It is not appropriate to exclude an incoming resource simply because it has not been spent in the same accounting period. It is quite normal in charities for funds to be raised first and then spent in accordance with a plan, such as with an appeal and other major fundraising activities. The unspent balance will be carried forward for future expenditure on the charitable objects. Since we are not trying to establish a 'profit' or 'loss', then the need to match income and expenditure in the financial accounts is not the same.

This will not apply to earned income of the charity, however, which should be treated in the same way as any commercial operation. A school receiving fees, for example, should treat early payment of fees as income received in advance. This would mean that the receipt is not included in income for the accounting period, but instead shown as received in advance under liabilities on the balance sheet, to be released into income in the appropriate accounting period.

In certain situations a charity may need to identify some voluntary income as received in advance of the balance sheet date. This will occur if the funding body has imposed specific terms that have to be met before the charity may use the funds. For example, a funding body may specify that a grant can only be spent in a certain timeframe that falls into a future accounting period. This is not the same as the normal delays that can occur between receipt of funds and the related expenditure. In the case where the terms of funding do impose pre-conditions, then the incoming resource should not be recognised in the SoFA until the conditions have been satisfied. If the funds have already been received, then they should be deferred as income received in advance.

The SORP requires incoming resources to be shown in the following categories:

- Donations, legacies and similar incoming resources
- Incoming resources from the operating activities of the charity, separating two main areas:
  - Activities in furtherance of the charity's objects
  - Activities for generating funds
- Investment income (including bank interest)
- Other incoming resources.

Charities may use headings that are appropriate to describe their activities, so it is not obligatory to use the exact words of those headings. However, it is necessary to reflect the split between those key areas. Charities are encouraged to use sub-headings to describe the activities generating incoming resources in more detail. It is common practice for the details of sources of funding to be included in the notes to the accounts, such as details of grant funders.

Where the charity undertakes some of its activities through a subsidiary company, the incoming resources will be included under the appropriate heading on consolidation. Similarly, branch activities should be brought into the appropriate income headings before deduction of expenses.

GIFTS IN KIND

Charities sometimes receive assets as donations, rather than cash. These can take several forms:

* Buildings or equipment donated to the charity for the charity's own use
* Equipment or supplies for the charity's own use
* Goods donated to charity shops or similar
* Goods for distribution.

Buildings or equipment donated to the charity for the charity's own use

These may be tangible fixed assets (*see Chapter 9 Tangible fixed assets*) if they are significant. If they are tangible fixed assets, then they need to be shown as an addition to fixed assets and depreciated in the same way as assets bought by the charity. As well as recognising the asset, the charity would recognise the same amount as an incoming resource in the SoFA in the same accounting period. This would usually form part of the restricted funds of the charity and the depreciation would be charged against the funds in the first and subsequent years (*see Chapter 7 Managing restricted funds*). Charities will have to estimate the value of such assets, possibly by asking the donor for an estimate. If an estimate is not available, then the charity should estimate the value of the donated asset by reference to an external source of information. For example, you might value a vehicle by reference to one of the published guides on second-hand vehicle prices.

Equipment or supplies for the charity's own use

Such donated goods may be smaller items of equipment that do not need to be classified as tangible fixed assets, or supplies to be used in operational activities. For example, a company may donate food normally sold in its stores, but which is just past its 'sell by' date, to a charity helping homeless people.

Donated goods should be valued at a reasonable estimate of their value to the charity. This may be the amount saved by the charity because it does not have to purchase the goods in cash, or it may be a lower amount if an estimate of the value can be made. As long as the method is reasonable and consistent, then this is acceptable. If it is a significant amount in the charity's accounts, then the basis of the valuation and any other relevant information should be included in the notes to the accounts.

If the amount of such donated goods is immaterial to the charity's accounts, then it does not have to be included at all.

The charity should show the value of donated goods as an incoming resource and show the same amount under expenditure under the relevant cost heading.

Goods donated to charity shops or similar

Many charities receive donations for resale in shops as second-hand goods. It is not practical to value these at the time of receipt and so it is acceptable to account only for the cash received once the goods have been sold. This applies in situations where the purpose of receiving the goods is to convert them into cash, or raise funds from them in some way.

A similar situation arises when charities receive donated goods for raffles, tombolas or auction at charity events. As the intention is to convert the donations into cash, then the charity only needs to recognise the funds raised.

Trustees should consider referring to the level of donated goods in their annual report where it is significant, as this may help a reader to understand the charity's activities.

Goods for distribution

Charities receive goods for onward distribution to their beneficiaries. For example, overseas development charities receive donated goods that they then distribute to people overseas.

Charities should include the donated goods under incoming resources as donations and the same amount under the relevant expenditure category. Both entries should be in the financial year in which the goods are distributed, avoiding the need to recognise stock in the balance sheet.

INTANGIBLE INCOME

Where services are donated to a charity, rather than goods, these are referred to as intangible income. Intangible income can be included in the SoFA in a similar way to donated goods, by including the value of the intangible income under donations and the relevant cost heading. It will be appropriate to include intangible income where the person donating the service has to bear the cost of providing the service, and the benefit is quantifiable and measurable. For example, a company providing a free payroll service or seconding staff to the charity.

Intangible income should be valued at the cost to the person providing the service. If this information is not available or the value to the charity is less than the cost to the third party, then the lower amount may be recognised in the SoFA. For example, a charity may be allowed to use premises in an expensive area free of charge. The charity therefore has intangible income valued at the amount of rent normally payable on those premises. However, this would distort the charity's SoFA if brought in on this valuation basis, as the charity would otherwise choose premises in a cheaper area, rather than pay such a high level of rent. The intangible income may therefore be valued on the basis of the rent level that the charity would expect to pay, representing the value to the charity of receiving rent-free premises.

Volunteer time is not recognised in charity accounts, although it should be recognised in the trustees' report. Giving time to charity does not generally represent a financial cost to volunteers, and it is difficult to measure the value.

RESOURCES EXPENDED

Normal accruals concepts apply to the recognition of expenditure for charities. Expenditure should only be recognised (and accrued if necessary) when the cost has been incurred before the end of the financial year. Charities should recognise legal obligations, making provisions where an obligation to pay at some future date has been established.

The categories of expenditure are:

◆ cost of generating funds
◆ charitable expenditure:
  – grants payable in furtherance of the charity's objects
  – costs of activities in furtherance of the charity's objects
  – support costs
  – management and administration of the charity.

Cost of generating funds

The costs of generating funds are the costs of obtaining funds for the charity's work, such as advertising, direct mail, staff time and agent's fees. It can include the costs of raising donations, and also the sales of goods or services if the purpose is to raise funds, such as selling Christmas cards. It will also include negotiating contracts or bids for new work, although the cost of monitoring and reporting progress on such contracts would usually be seen as part of the support costs of the work funded by the contract.

Publicity to raise the charity's profile should be included in this category, but not advertising to promote the charity's objects or to educate people about the cause. For example, advertising to recruit volunteers or new pupils to a school should be seen as part of the charitable activities of the charity. Advertising a jumble sale to raise funds would be part of the cost of generating funds. Publicity to promote the charity's objects is likely to be targeted at beneficiaries or others who can use the information to further the charity's objectives.

Information targeted at potential donors (rather than potential beneficiaries) should be part of the cost of generating funds, even where it provides general information about the charity's activities.

Fundraising costs should not be netted off against income. Where a branch or a subsidiary company is used to undertake some of the charity's fundraising activities, the costs of those activities would have to be included under the cost of generating funds in the consolidated SoFA.

Investment management fees are included under the cost of generating funds.

Charitable expenditure

Charitable expenditure comprises all expenditure directly relating to the objects of the charity. It should include grants payable and costs of activities in furtherance of the charity's objects.

Grants payable

Where grantmaking is a significant activity to the charity, then the SoFA should show grants payable as a line and show the amounts distributed. The administrative costs of grantmaking will be shown under support costs or management and administration.

Costs of activities in furtherance of the charity's objects

These costs will include the direct costs of supporting charitable activities and projects (for example, salaries, office, communications and other costs identifiable as an integral part of the cost of carrying out those charitable activities or projects), as well as depreciation of fixed assets where used wholly or mainly for charitable activities. The charity should describe the main charitable activities and attribute expenditure to them to give an indication of the way resources are expended. This should mirror the activities shown under the incoming resources categories as far as possible. A note to the accounts will give further analysis of the expenditure.

Support costs

Support costs are part of the charitable expenditure and may be the management of projects from a central office. Support costs may be attributed to the charity's activities as an integral part of the cost of providing those services. However, if material, support costs should be shown separately on the face of the SoFA.

Management and administration of the charity

Costs of managing and administering the charity will include direct costs incurred in organisational administration and complying with statutory requirements. For example, the cost of audit and trustees' meetings would be management and administration of the charity. However, there will also be some staff time and office costs that should be apportioned to this category. Note that the management of the charity's *projects* (rather than the management of the organisation) should be treated as a support cost.

As well as showing the expenditure under these headings on the face of the SoFA, you need to describe the expenditure in 'natural' headings in the notes to the accounts. These are the categories of rent, rates, salaries and so on that we are accustomed to in ordinary accounts. The notes should also show how the totals on the SoFA are constituted.

FUND ACCOUNTING

One of the other major aspects of charity accounts is that all incoming and outgoing resources, assets and liabilities belong to a fund in the charity's accounts. It is necessary to track funds through the accounts, so that one knows the amounts received, expended and balances on each type of fund. The different types of funds are:

- restricted funds, which can comprise of:
  - permanent endowment funds
  - expendable endowment funds
  - restricted income funds
- unrestricted funds, which can comprise of:
  - general funds
  - designated funds.

Restricted funds

Restricted funds are funds subject to special trusts specified by the donor. This might be because it was a public appeal for a specific purpose, or grants or donations where the donor has specified what they wish the funds to be spent on. For example, a grant to fund a project of the charity would be restricted income. Income may also be restricted because the donor wishes the funds to be used to help the charity's beneficiaries in a particular geographical area. Restricted funds may also include land, buildings or other assets donated to a charity. The trustees will be in breach of trust if they use restricted income other than for the specified purpose. This is an important legal requirement that must be reflected in the accounts.

Permanent endowment funds

Permanent endowment funds are donations that have been given to a charity to be held as capital with no power to convert the funds to income. These may be cash or other assets. This means that the charity has to hold these funds intact in perpetuity, investing them to earn income. Usually the income arising will be unrestricted income, unless the terms of the original endowment impose restrictions on the use of the funds.

Expendable endowment funds

Expendable endowment funds are donations that have been given to a charity to be held as capital, where the trustees do have a discretionary power to use the funds as income. The terms of the original endowment may set out the circumstances for the funds to be expended, or activities that may be funded.

Restricted income funds

Restricted income funds are funds received for a particular purpose to be spent in accordance with the wishes of the donor. Restricted income funds may be raised through an appeal, donations or grants and may be in the form of assets rather than cash.

The presumption underlying a restricted fund is that any interest or other investment income earned on a restricted fund will be added to the fund. This will only apply to material amounts. In some cases the terms of the donation will state how investment income should be applied.

Unrestricted funds

Unrestricted funds are funds available for the purposes of the charity, to be spent as the trustees see fit.

General funds

General funds are unrestricted funds that have not been earmarked and may be used generally to further the charity's objects.

Designated funds

Designated funds are unrestricted funds that have been earmarked for a particular purpose by the trustees. The notes to the accounts should explain the purpose of designated funds.

STATEMENT OF FINANCIAL ACTIVITIES (SoFA)

The SoFA draws together information on incoming resources and resources expended, replacing the income and expenditure account (or profit and loss account) as a primary statement in the financial statements. The SoFA needs to be presented in columnar form, showing the funds of the charity as appropriate. It is usual for the various restricted income funds to be grouped together into one column, with further explanation in the notes to the accounts. Designated funds do not have to be shown separately on the face of the SoFA as they are part of the unrestricted funds. The charity may, however, add further columns to identify designated funds or specific restricted funds if this helps to explain the financial position of the charity.

	Unrestricted funds	Restricted funds	Endowment funds	This year total	Last year total
Incoming resources					
Resources expended					
Net incoming resources					
Funds brought forward at beginning of year					
Funds carried forward at end of year					

The SORP requires charities to identify the assets and liabilities that form each fund. This can be done by way of a note to the accounts, or the balance sheet can be presented in a columnar format.

Transfers between funds

Charities may need to makes transfers from one fund to another and this should be shown on the SoFA below the net incoming resources. This may occur for a variety of reasons, such as a transfer from endowment to unrestricted funds. Transfers should not be netted off against each other and they should be explained in notes to the accounts, quoting the authority if any was needed for the transfer.

Revaluations

Charities have to revalue their investments to market value each year, showing the gain or loss on revaluation after transfers in the SoFA. Similarly, they may choose to revalue property occupied by the charity.

Unincorporated charities may now combine the realised and unrealised gains on their investments into one line. Charitable companies should note that they are still obliged to identify the unrealised gains separately. Indeed, the revaluation fund should be disclosed separately on the face of the balance sheet.

Funds brought forward and funds carried forward

At the foot of the SoFA, the overall position on funds is drawn together to match the balance sheet, giving the closing funds position.

The requirement to account for the separate funds of a charity is one of the most important aspects of the SORP. The fund analysis in the SoFA will focus on the balance between restricted and unrestricted funds in a charity. To maintain financial health, a charity must have adequate unrestricted fund balances.

Example: Statement of Financial Activities (incorporating an income and expenditure account) for the year ended 31 March 2002

	Restricted £	Unrestricted £	2002 Total £	2001 Total £
Incoming resources				
Activities to further charity's objects	150,000	95,535	**245,535**	207,304
Activities to generate funds				
Charity shop		19,465	**19,465**	17,242
Donations	5,000	-	**5,000**	6,796
Investment income	765	900	**1,665**	1,324
Total incoming resources	**155,765**	**115,900**	**271,665**	**232,666**
Resources expended				
Cost of generating funds				
Charity shop	-	14,773	**14,773**	11,225
Fundraising and publicity	-	4,079	**4,079**	1,893
Charitable expenditure				
Advice and information	67,008	-	**67,008**	59,876
Outreach work	68,391	-	**68,391**	53,316
Training project	-	80,836	**80,836**	63,606
Management & administration of the charity	1,250	8,827	**10,077**	7,372
Total resources expended	**136,649**	**108,515**	**245,164**	**197,288**
Net income for the year	**19,116**	**7,385**	**26,501**	**35,378**
Unrealised gain on investments	-	762	762	202
Net movement in funds	**19,116**	**8,147**	**27,263**	**35,580**
Funds at 1 April 2001	1,316	20,249	21,565	(14,015)
Funds at 31 March 2002	**20,432**	**28,396**	**48,828**	**21,565**

All of the above results are derived from continuing activities. There were no other recognised gains or losses other than those stated above. Movements in funds are disclosed in note x to the financial statements.

BALANCE SHEET

A charity balance sheet is very similar to a balance sheet for any commercial entity. Financial Reporting Standards apply to charities as they do to other entities.

Investments should be valued at market value at the balance sheet date and the revaluation difference taken to the appropriate fund.

The assets and liabilities making up a fund should be identified. Charities may choose to provide a fund analysis on the face of the balance sheet, using a columnar format; however, most charities provide this information in the notes to the accounts.

SUMMARY INCOME AND EXPENDITURE ACCOUNT

Charitable companies have to comply with the Companies Act with regard to the format and content of their annual accounts, as well as the SORP. The Companies Act requires an income and expenditure account to show the revenue income to the organisation. A charity including non-revenue items, such as a new endowment in the incoming resources, will therefore need to prepare a separate statement in addition to the SoFA.

This may be necessary where the SoFA includes:

◆ new endowment funds in the year or transfers between endowment and general funds

◆ unrealised gains or losses

◆ discontinued activities.

The summary income and expenditure account needs to exclude new endowments, but include transfers from endowment to revenue funds. It also needs to exclude unrealised gains. FRS 3 requires the separation of continuing and discontinued activities. It can be easier to comply with this requirement in the summary income and expenditure account instead of the SoFA. The summary income and expenditure account does not require an analysis by fund, so columns showing the different types of funds of the charity are not necessary.

Not all charities will need to do a summary income and expenditure account. If a charity only has unrealised gains, but no endowment funds, then it is possible to present the information in the SoFA in such a way that complies with the requirements of the SORP and Companies Act.

This can be achieved by ensuring that there is a clear sub-total identifying the net income or net expenditure for the year. This should come before the unrealised gains are brought into the SoFA. An example of this layout follows. Note that the title of the statement should include reference to the fact that the income and expenditure accounts are incorporated into the SoFA.

Example format for a summary income and expenditure account

	Continuing operations	Discontinued operations	Total
Income			
Income from grants, donations, trading			
Investment income			
Surplus/(deficit) on the disposal of tangible fixed assets			
Net realised gains/(losses) on the disposal of investments			
Transfer from endowment fund			
Total income			
Total expenditure			
Surplus/(deficit) for the year Funds brought forward			
Funds carried forward			

CASHFLOW STATEMENT

A cashflow statement is required by FRS 1 in the financial statements of larger charities. Smaller charities are exempt and the thresholds for qualification as small are those set out in the Companies Act relating to various reporting requirements.

A small charity for the purposes of FRS 1 compliance is one that can comply with two out of three of the following conditions:

◆ Gross income not exceeding £2.8m
◆ Balance sheet total (gross assets, not net assets) not exceeding £1.4m
◆ Average number of employees not exceeding 50.

For unincorporated Scottish charities, the thresholds are set down in the Law Reform (Miscellaneous Provisions) (Scotland) Act 1990, and are £2m gross income and £975,000 gross assets.

The objective of a cashflow statement is to show the cash received and applied by the charity in the financial year.

Example: Cashflow Statement

	Note	2002 Total £'000	2001 Total £'000
Net cash inflow from operating activities	1	9,845	621
Purchase of fixed assets		(55)	0
Returns on investments and servicing of finance	2	222	241
Movement in net funds in the year	3	10,012	862
Net funds at 1 April 2001		2,856	1,994
Net funds at 31 March 2002		**12,868**	**2,856**

1. Reconciliation of operating surplus to net cash inflow from operating activities

Net incoming resources	329	128
Depreciation	92	79
Inflow from investments, etc.	(222)	(241)
Increase in creditors	9,609	684
Decrease\(increase) in debtors	36	(29)
Decrease in stocks	1	0
Net cash inflow from operating activities	**9,845**	**621**

2. Analysis of cash flows for headings netted in the cashflow statement

Interest received	202	171
Income from subsidiary	20	70
Returns on investment and servicing of finance	**222**	**241**

3. Analysis of changes in net funds

As at 1 April 2001	2,856	1,994
Cashflow	10,012	862
As at 31 March 2002	**12,868**	**2,856**

Source: National Association of Victim Support Schemes Annual Report and Accounts for the year ended 31 March 2002

NOTES TO THE ACCOUNTS

All charities will need to provide some notes to provide further explanation and details on items included in the main financial statements. The notes are part of the financial statements and will be reviewed as part of the audit.

At a minimum, charities need to include the items required by the SORP, but charities should also add further information where they think this improves a reader's understanding of the accounts. Charities need to consider the financial statements as part of their communication with the public and their funders and donors, and it is therefore in their own interests to provide adequate information, rather than simply the minimum required.

ACCOUNTING POLICIES

All charities will need to provide details of their accounting policies. These describe the basis on which the accounts are drawn up. Charities should explain their policies for:

- recognising income, especially when they would defer income and other special circumstances
- dealing with gifts in kind and intangible income
- recording liabilities and expenditure
- the basis for allocating costs
- the funds held by the charity and how they are recognised and accounted for
- revaluing assets
- capitalising and depreciating tangible fixed assets
- dealing with transactions in foreign currencies
- handling lease arrangements if applicable
- handling pension costs if applicable
- any other matter relevant to the business and financial statement of that particular charity; for example, if they have stock, then a policy will be needed for the accounting treatment of stock.

Many of these policies will be the same each year and charities do not need to radically change their policies every year. In addition, many policies will be similar to other similar charities. It is therefore useful to review the example accounts in the Charity Commission publication CC66 for guidance on wording and the full range of accounting policies that may be needed.

2 ▼ Trustees' annual report

As well as annual accounts, registered charities (and excepted charities if requested) must prepare an annual report, which has to be submitted to the Charity Commission together with the accounts. This requirement applies to charitable companies as well as unincorporated charities. However, companies may incorporate the information required under the Companies Act for the directors' report into the trustees' annual report.

Very small charities with a gross income or total expenditure not exceeding £10,000 do not have to prepare and file an annual report. Charities with gross income or total expenditure over £250,000 have to provide a fuller report. The requirements are contained in *The Charities (Accounts and Reports) Regulations 2000* and the SORP, and summarised in CC61 published by the Charity Commission.

Requirements for annual reports of all charities

◆ The financial year to which the report relates.

◆ Legal and administrative details (see below).

◆ A brief summary of the main activities and achievements of the charity during the year in relation to the charity's objects.

◆ Reserves policy (*see Chapter 4*).

◆ Investment policy, where applicable (*see Chapter 5*).

◆ Grant-making policy, where applicable (*see Chapter 6*).

◆ Relationships with other charities or organisations with which the charity cooperates to achieve its objectives.

◆ A statement of the trustees' responsibilities in relation to the accounts and accounting matters. This is a requirement for all financial statements on which auditors provide an opinion.

◆ Date the report is approved, with the signature of at least one trustee who is authorised to sign on behalf of the trustees.

The legal and administrative details may be put onto one page before the narrative sections of the trustees' annual report.

Legal and administrative details to be included in annual report

- The name of the charity as it appears in the register of charities and any ot which it makes itself known.
- The charity registration number and company number.
- Principal address of the charity and registered office of a company.
- Details of governing instrument, such as the nature of the document and date established.
- Objects of the charity.
- Details of any restrictions imposed by governing document.
- A summary of any specific investment powers and their authority (for example, governing document or Charity Commission order).
- Names of advisers, such as investment managers, bankers, solicitors and auditors.
- Names of trustees during the year and at the date the report is signed (or a minimum of 50 trustees if there are more than 50 trustees).
- The method by which trustees are appointed.
- The name of any other person or body entitled to appoint one or more of the charity trustees.
- The name of any other person holding property on behalf of the charity, i.e. acting as a trustee.

The responsibility for the preparation of the annual report rests with the trustees. The language in the report may be amended to reflect the governance structure adopted by the charity. For example, the charity may refer to their trustees as directors, and may use terms such as management committee or council of management to refer to the governing body. The trustees are all responsible for the annual report and therefore it should be approved at a normal trustees' meeting, following the procedure of the charity for such matters.

Larger charities (those with gross income exceeding £250,000) need to provide a fuller narrative report as well as a statement confirming that the trustees have reviewed the major risks facing the charity and established systems to mitigate those risks. The processes for reviewing risks are examined in more detail in Chapter 3 Risk Assessment.

Additional requirements for charities with gross income of more than £250,000

- A longer review of activities and a strategy to replace the brief review.
- The organisational structure of the charity (for example, whether it has branches).
- Commentary on significant changes, developments and achievements in the past year.
- Description of any significant events since the end of the year and any likely future developments.
- An explanation of any funds in deficit and the action taken or planned to eradicate the deficit.
- A statement confirming that the major risks to which the charity is exposed have been reviewed and systems have been established to mitigate those risks.
- As well as the investment policy, larger charities should comment on the performance of investments over the past financial year.

Charities can use the trustees' annual report as an opportunity to explain the work of the charity and its objectives, strategy and achievements. The most effective annual reports can be linked easily to the statement of financial activities by describing the main incoming resources and items of expenditure. Unusual items in the financial statements should be explained, as well as some of the non-financial matters that may be relevant. For example, the level of support given to the charity by volunteers can be described in the annual report. Gifts in kind and intangible income can also be described here, even if included in the financial statements. Significant intangible income that is not included in the financial statements should be described in the annual report.

An example of a charity using the trustees' annual report to explain the work and achievements of the charity is given below.

Example:

The council of management presents its report on the audited financial statements for the year ended 31 March 2001.

Basis and values

Waste Watch is a charity whose inspiration and values derive from a desire to protect the environment by ensuring the sustainable use and disposal of scarce resources, primarily by advocating waste reduction, reuse and recycling of materials – the 3Rs. These values provide the basis of our work with community and voluntary organisations, local authorities, educational institutions, businesses and individual members of the public, all of whom share our desire for an improved environment and the reduction of waste.

Objects

The objects of Waste Watch as defined by the memorandum of association are:

- to advance public education about all aspects of waste generation, waste management and waste recycling, and;

◆ to preserve and protect the physical and natural environment for the public benefit through the promotion of waste reduction, reuse, reclamation and recycling of waste materials.

Focus of Waste Watch work in 2000–2001

During 2000–2001, Waste Watch's work covered the following areas:

◆ Research and policy
◆ Providing information and advice
◆ Working with schools
◆ Membership.

Research and policy

As the leading national organisation campaigning on issues around waste reduction, reuse and recycling, Waste Watch places great importance on effective and innovative research and dialogue with policy makers. As such we carried out a major research project – Beyond the Bin – which looked at the real costs of different methods of waste disposal. This was distributed widely to key policy makers through a printed summary report and also a full report on the Waste Watch website. Other policy work included giving evidence to regional and national government committees and gaining more than 400 signatures for the Manifesto for Market Development – aimed at showing widespread support for the need for government action to support markets for recycled products during the development of the government's Waste Strategy 2000. The government's focus on development of the Waste and Resources Action Programme demonstrated that market development had moved up the political agenda.

Objectives

◆ To deliver research on key issues to appropriate policy-makers and partners.
◆ To contribute to the development of waste strategies that incorporate the aims of Waste Watch.
◆ To provide support for the National Waste Awareness Initiative (NWAI) in the form of managing a co-ordinator post and a research project into effective communication of recycling messages.

Achievements

◆ Beyond the Bin executive summaries produced and circulated to key decision makers. A pdf of the full report was made available on the Waste Watch website and accessed by 1,992 people.
◆ Ray Georgeson, Executive Director, seconded to the DETR (now DEFRA) in an advisory capacity.
◆ Waste Watch continued to contribute to the development of waste strategies both locally and nationally. This included giving evidence to the Greater London Assembly's Waste Recycling Investigative Committee Hearing.
◆ NWAI research was completed in November 2001 and presented to the Parliamentary Sustainable Waste Group, and through four presentations in London, Plymouth, Newcastle and Wolverhampton.
◆ A Manifesto for Market Development was submitted to the DETR. The manifesto suggested seven points for action following the report of the DETR's Market Development Group. The manifesto gained the support of more than 400 key representatives across all sectors concerned with waste and recycling.

Providing information and advice

Waste Watch is committed to providing information and advice of the highest quality to all sectors of the community. A key component of this is 'Wasteline', a telephone and web-based helpline run from the Waste Watch offices. Since the development of the website, the number of people using this service has increased dramatically from 38,500 in 1998 to 152,306 in 2000.

During 2000–2001, Waste Watch also completed the two year 3Rs for the 3rd Sector project, which aimed to give people working in community and not-for-profit organisations the tools to introduce waste reduction, reuse and recycling policies into their organisations. Waste Watch also delivers information and advice through training events and publications.

Waste Watch works to raise awareness of its work and the 3Rs message through proactive media relations. One of the highlights of the year was the appearance of projects officer Jim Fielder in two television items showing how people can reduce the amount of waste they produce. An appearance on the BBC South East's Trash City, a programme following a family who tries to practice the 3Rs for a week, led to a live interview on the national GMTV about the 3Rs.

Objectives

◆ Wasteline to respond to 7,500 post and phone enquiries.

◆ The information section of the Waste Watch website to receive 20,000 visits.

◆ Wasteline to produce two new information sheets during the year.

◆ Achieve 200 media articles in the year.

Achievements

◆ Wasteline received 6,887 post and phone enquiries.

◆ The information section of the Waste Watch website received 152,306 hits.

◆ New information sheets produced on European Waste and Recycling in London.

◆ Achieved 405 media articles and responded to 123 press enquiries.

Working with schools

Waste Watch runs a highly regarded programme of work for teachers and children in primary and secondary schools in the UK. Work with schools aims to provide educational opportunities around the 3Rs, tied in to the National Curriculum. The Dustbin Pack is a free pack for teachers of 7 to 11 year-olds packed with worksheets, teachers notes and posters.

ReCyclerbility features Cycler the rapping robot which visits schools around the country with a recycling rap aimed at entertaining children while teaching them about the 3Rs. Cycler is actually three robots and their outreach workers Geoff Collett, Wendy Jenkinson and Dave Taggart.

Schools Waste Action Clubs (SWACs) are based in local authority areas and aim to promote waste activities in schools that meet National Curriculum targets in areas such as geography, maths, science and citizenship. The project encourages children to examine their own school's waste and find solutions such as waste-free lunches and paper recycling, to reduce the amount of waste going to landfill.

Finally, the education team delivers training for people who work with schools on environmental issues through Work at Waste at School training days.

Objectives

◆ Revise Dustbin Pack and print 5,000 copies, distributing 1,000 by the end of the year.

- Cycler the robot to visit 100,000 schoolchildren at 650 schools.
- Launch new Schools Waste Action Clubs following on from successful pilot projects in Stockport and York.
- Deliver two Work at Waste at School training days.

Achievements

- 5,000 Dustbin Packs printed and 1,372 distributed to schools.
- Three school outreach workers visited 72,119 schoolchildren with Cycler the rapping robot and presented 538 shows.
- Schools Waste Action Clubs launched in Suffolk, Norfolk, Essex and the London Borough of Bexley.
- Two Work at Waste at School training days held.

Membership

Waste Watch's members come from all sectors of the community including small and large businesses, local authorities, national and local community organisations and individuals. Members are important for the governance of Waste Watch, which is achieved through the annual general meeting. All the Waste Watch trustees are members of Waste Watch.

Objectives

- Increase membership by 50.
- Carry out survey of members.
- Explore new membership services.
- Publish four editions of Waste Watch Review, our members' newsletter.
- Hold the Waste Watch AGM and Annual Lecture.

Achievements

- We gained 56 new members during this period through a membership drive based around a new membership leaflet and a request to members to recommend Waste Watch membership to others. However, as some existing members chose not to renew their membership during this period the number of members we had at 31st March 2001 was 400, a decrease of four on the previous year's figure of 404.
- A survey carried out December–March 2001 achieved a 22% response rate and was overwhelmingly positive about membership of Waste Watch with 64% saying they would definitely recommend membership and 32% possibly recommending it. No one said they wouldn't recommend membership. A report on the questionnaire was featured in Waste Watch Review – Summer 2001 Edition 9.
- We set up a membership group to explore membership relations from renewals through to new services. The members survey showed that 62.5% of members would like to receive information via e-mail rather than through the post, which has led to Waste Watch developing new members services.
- We published four editions of Waste Watch Review newsletter which our survey found had 82% readership.
- The annual general meeting held in September 2000 attracted members and was followed by the Waste Watch Annual Seminar whose speaker this year was Ludwig Kramer, the head of the EU Waste Strategy Unit.

Waste Watch organisation and corporate governance

Waste Watch is a company limited by guarantee and a registered charity. Its governing instrument is the memorandum and articles of association as adopted by the resolution passed on the 18 September 1991. Its governing body is a council of management, whose members are elected by the members of the company and nominees from the previous council of management.

On 31 March 2001 the council of management comprised 11 members. The council of management meets four times a year, and is assisted by one committee – the finance and personnel sub-committee, which meets bi-monthly and comprises of four council members, including the chair and treasurer. This committee oversees financial management and the conduct of personnel and equal opportunities matters. It reports to the full council of management at its quarterly meetings. Full council meetings consider reports from the executive director, and guide the executive director and other officers on the implementation of policies and courses of action, and considers recommendations for action from the executive director.

All members of the council of management have access to the advice and services of the company secretary.

Objectives

- To complete and implement the Waste Watch pay and benefits review.
- To work towards developing a five-year strategy for Waste Watch.
- To hold a staff 'Away Day' for team-building and creating a greater knowledge of the organisation and wider issues in our field.

Achievements

- Pay and benefits review completed and first staff appraisals carried out under the new system in March 2001.
- Strategy development started with meetings involving the council of management and management team.
- Staff Away Day held 4–6 July.

Source: Waste Watch Report and Financial Statements 2001

FUNDS HELD AS CUSTODIAN TRUSTEE

Where a charity is holding funds as custodian trustee, then it should not include those funds in its balance sheet, but should provide information on this activity both in the notes to the financial statements and in the trustees' annual report. The information should include:

- a description of the assets held;
- the objects of the charity on whose behalf the assets are held and how this activity falls within their own objects;
- details of the arrangements for safe custody and segregation of such assets from the charity's own assets.

SUMMARISED FINANCIAL INFORMATION

Many charities produce summarised financial information for inclusion in another report or annual review intended for wider circulation, such as to donors and supporters. The SORP reminds trustees that any such summarised financial information should always be fair and accurate.

The guidance in the charity SORP describes two levels of summaries:

- summarised financial information, limited in its content
- summarised financial statements, containing information on both the SoFA and the balance sheet.

For either level, the summaries can be simple extracts and include such representations as graphs, tables and pie charts.

Summarised financial information

A summary in any form that does not contain information from both the SoFA and the balance sheet must be accompanied by a statement signed on behalf of the trustees to explain the purpose of the information, and to state whether it is from the full statutory report and accounts. It should also state whether they have been audited or examined, and give details of how the full statutory report and accounts may be obtained.

Example: Trustees' statement

The summarised financial information shows the income raised for our activities, the cost of raising the income and the amounts spent on our charitable activities. The information is taken from the full financial statements, which were approved by the trustees on [date]. In order to gain a full understanding of the financial affairs of the charity, the full audited financial statements, trustees' annual report and auditors' report should be consulted. Copies can be obtained from the charity.

Signed on behalf of the trustees

Summarised financial statements

Summarised financial statements should contain information from both the balance sheet and the SoFA and should be a fair summary of the financial statements. If necessary, trustees should consider whether information contained in the notes to the financial statements should be included in order to provide sufficient information. Summarised financial statements should be accompanied by a statement, signed on behalf of the trustees, indicating:

- that they are not the statutory accounts but a summary of information relating to both the SoFA and the balance sheet

- whether the full financial statements have been audited or examined, and whether the report was unqualified

- if the opinion was qualified, enough details should be provided to enable the reader to appreciate the significance of the report

- if the summary relates to a branch, then the financial information should be an extract from the full financial statements and the main charity name should be given

- the date on which the trustees approved the annual accounts

- whether the statutory report and accounts have been submitted to the Charity Commission and, for charitable companies, to Companies House

- where the full financial statements can be obtained.

Example: Statement required from the trustees

These summarised financial statements contain information from both the Statement of Financial Activities and the balance sheet for the year ended 31 December 2001, but are not the full statutory report and accounts. The full financial statements were approved by the trustees on [day/month/year] and subsequently submitted to the Charity Commission [and to Companies House]. They received an unqualified audit report and copies may be obtained from the charity's head office.

Signed on behalf of the trustees
[Name/position/date]

The auditors may be asked to provide an opinion on whether the summarised financial statements are a fair summary. Auditors have to follow Audit Practice Note 11 issued by the Auditing Practices Board. In the guidance, auditors are advised to use the following wording for an opinion on summarised financial statements.

Example: Auditors' statement on summarised financial statements

Independent auditors' statement to the trustees of [charity name].

We have examined the summarised financial statements of [charity name].

Respective responsibilities of trustees and auditors

The trustees are responsible for preparing the summarised financial statements in accordance with the recommendations of the charities SORP.

Our responsibility is to report to you our opinion on the consistency of the summarised financial statements with the full financial statements and trustees' annual report. We also read the other information contained in the annual report [review] and consider the implications for our report if we become aware of any apparent misstatements or material inconsistencies with the summarised financial statements.

Basis of opinion

We conducted our work in accordance with Bulletin 1999/6, The auditors' statement on the summary financial statement, issued by the Auditing Practices Board for use in the United Kingdom.

Opinion

In our opinion the summarised financial statements are consistent with the full financial statements and the trustees' annual report of [charity name] for the year ended 31 December 2001.

Registered Auditors

Date

---

3 ▼ Risk assessment

The Statement of Recommended Practice: Accounting and Reporting by Charities (SORP 2000), published in October 2000, requires a statement in the trustees' annual report to confirm that the trustees have assessed risks to the charity each year.

> *A statement confirming that the major risks to which the charity is exposed, as identified by the trustees, have been reviewed and systems have been established to mitigate those risks.*
>
> SORP 2000 paragraph 31 (g)

Smaller charities with gross income below £250,000 do not have to provide the statement as it is not required by the Charities (Accounts and Reports) Regulations 2000 ('the regulations').

In order to make the statement, the charity needs to work through three steps to:
- identify the risks
- prioritise them
- establish what action needs to be taken in relation to the risks.

STEP 1 • IDENTIFYING THE RISKS

Risk can be defined as uncertainties surrounding opportunities and threats that have the potential to enhance or inhibit performance, the achievement of objectives and the meeting of stakeholder expectations. In other words, a risk can be anything that has the potential to prevent you from reaching your goal. For charities and organisations, it can be very helpful if the risk identification process is rooted in the objectives of the charity. However, risk is also about taking appropriate risks to achieve objectives and should be about identifying opportunities as well as negative risks.

Starting from the charity's objectives, the charity should think about the risks that might prevent the charity from achieving those objectives. This will produce a 'top level' review of risks, looking at the overall scene both inside the charity and externally.

As prompts for identifying risks, it may be helpful to think in terms of:
- failure to ...
- loss of ...
- concentration of ...
- non-compliance with ...
- lack of ...
- reduction of ...
- conflict between ...
- inability to ...
- inappropriate ...
- reliance on ...
- disruption to ...
- inadequate ...
- increase in ...
- delay in ...

For example, the loss of funding from a major donor would pose a significant threat to the continuation of the charity's work in a particular field.

In generating the list of risks, it is important to consider threats *and* the consequences of the threats materialising. If it were identified that the charity is reliant on funding from one source, then that in itself does not articulate a risk. It is necessary to consider the consequences of that particular aspect. For this example, the risk may be that the funder is able to specify the purpose for which the funds should be spent, which in turn could take the charity in a direction that is not well matched to the strategic direction it has chosen.

Categories of risk

When identifying risks in Step 1, you need to think widely about internal and external factors that could affect the charity. The major risks to the charity are not likely to be only financial risks. Consider the following categories:

- people
- operational
- financial
- strategic
- funding
- social
- competition
- management
- information
- property
- reputation
- regulatory
- technological
- political
- governance
- natural.

So, for example, a charity may identify a risk of flooding to their premises.

STEP 2 • ASSESSING THE RISKS

Once the risks have been identified, and it is very likely that there will be an extensive list, the risks need to be assessed. The key factors are:

- probability
- impact
- level of concern.

Probability refers to the likelihood that a threat will materialise. Impact relates to the effect that would be felt if the event did occur. Probability or likelihood and impact or effect are the common factors seen in all descriptions of risk assessment.

In Step 2, experience has shown that it can be helpful to use a third measure, which is usually called 'level of concern'. This is a way of drawing out people's perceptions about a particular risk, and this additional measure will weight the priority ranking to risks that receive a high score on level of concern as well as probability and impact.

A scoring system should be agreed. One system is:

Probability	Impact	Level of concern
1 = very unlikely	1 = insignificant	1 = unconcerned
2 = unlikely	2 = fairly serious	2 = mildly concerned
3 = possible	3 = serious	3 = concerned
4 = likely	4 = very serious	4 = very concerned
5 = highly likely	5 = major disaster	5 = gravely concerned

Alternatively, a simple high, medium or low analysis could be used.

There is no need for a pretence that this process is entirely objective; it is subjective and each person will come to different conclusions about the perception of a particular risk. Undertaking this as a collective exercise will focus the organisation's attention on a key issue: *risk appetite*. One person might score a potential event as low probability, whereas another person may perceive the risk as highly likely. The process of assessing the risks can be a very positive exercise in sharing the different perceptions of risk. As part of the process the organisation should come to a reasonable consensus about the level and types of risks it is prepared to accept. This process may take some time and risk assessment may have to be revisited several times.

Multiply the scores, from your scoring system (above), to produce the priority ranking:

	Probability	Impact	Concern	Total
Database crash	4	3	4	48
Key person leaves	3	2	2	12
New procedure fails	4	3	3	36

Using these factors you can prioritise the risks, so that the long list becomes more manageable. The focus moves to the risks with the highest ranking.

If you prefer, you can map the scores for probability and impact to provide a graphic illustration of key areas of risk:

IMPACT	high impact low probability	high impact high probability
	low impact low probability	low impact high probability

PROBABILITY

As an example, the above table showing the prioritised risks would be illustrated on such a map as follows:

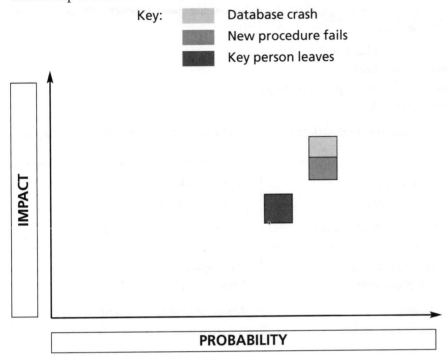

In order to include the level of concern, you may choose to draw a risk map as a bubble diagram, where the size of the bubbles illustrates the level of concern.

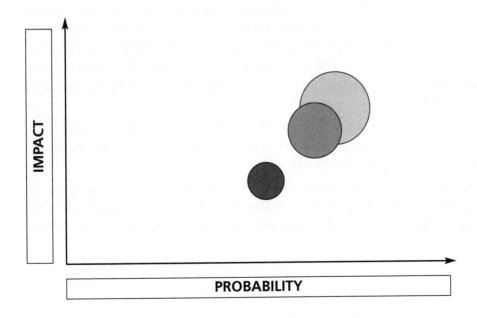

STEP 3 • ESTABLISHING ACTION POINTS

Appropriate action will depend on the nature of the risk. Consider:

- avoiding the activity
- minimising the likelihood
- mitigating the effects
- transfering the risk (e.g. by insuring)
- accepting the risk.

In general terms, the appropriate actions for the four quadrants on the risk map are:

IMPACT

high impact low probability *Mitigate effects/transfer*	high impact high probability *Avoid/minimise likelihood*
low impact low probability *Accept*	low impact high probability *Minimise likelihood/accept*

PROBABILITY

Where the probability is high for an internal risk, then the charity can take action to minimise the likelihood. Where the probability is high for an external risk, then there is little the charity can do to prevent the threat materialising. The charity therefore has to consider whether it can manage the situation if the event did happen, which is about mitigating the effects of an event, or whether it has to cease the activity to avoid the risk altogether.

The charity will also have to consider the level of risk that it is prepared to accept. If the risks are known and managed, then this is a good outcome for the charity. In this situation, no further action may be required.

The charity will also need to balance the cost of controlling the risk against the cost of mitigating the risk should the threat materialise. The cost of controls needs to be proportionate to the risk and the aim is not to eliminate all risks, but to manage them.

RISK REGISTER

A register draws together the key information for the highest priority risks:

- Clear identification of the risk.
- Consequences of that risk becoming a reality.
- Action required to deal with the risk. This should identify the timescale and responsibility for the action. This will then need to be monitored.

Risk	Consequences	
Database containing names of all members crashes.	Loss of income. Damage to relationship with members.	

Actions	Who	Timescale
Ensure database is backed up daily.	Staff	By end July
Ensure contract with IT support company is valid and provides for immediate action.	Staff	By end Aug
Provide IT training for membership team.	Staff	By end Sept

MONITORING AND REASSESSMENT

In order to reap the benefits of risk assessment, risk review needs to be brought into the cyclical planning process of the charity and be embedded within the processes of the charity. Regular review will ensure that the trustees and management are aware of the current risks facing the charity. These will change, as will the extent of exposure to them.

RISK STATEMENT IN TRUSTEES' ANNUAL REPORT

Having established a system for assessing and monitoring risk, and implementing action to improve systems and controls as a result of the risk assessment, trustees will be able to make the statement in the trustees' annual report as required by the SORP.

Example: Risk management

The trustees actively review the major risks which the charity faces on a regular basis and believe that maintaining our free reserves at the levels stated above, combined with our annual review of the controls over key financial systems carried out through an internal audit programme, will provide sufficient resources in the event of adverse conditions. The trustees have also examined other operational and business risks which we face and confirm that they have established systems to mitigate the significant risks.

Source: CC66 SORP 2000: Example Reports and Accounts

Example: Risk review

The management committee has conducted its own review of the major risks to which the charity is exposed and systems have been established to mitigate those risks. Significant external risks to funding have led to the development of a strategic plan, which will allow for the diversification of funding and activities. Internal risks are minimised by the implementation of procedures for authorisation of all transactions and projects and to ensure consistent quality of delivery for all operational aspects of the charitable company. These procedures are periodically reviewed to ensure that they still meet the needs of the charity.

Source: CC66 SORP 2000: Example Reports and Accounts

You may feel that it is enough to simply comply with the SORP. However, the benefits of the process may well assist the charity in its governance and management. Risk assessment processes can:

- provide a structured way of dealing with current and future risks
- create the right culture so that the charity can learn from mistakes and take advantage of opportunities
- help to focus decision-making and actions on the priority issues for the charity emanating from the charity's objectives
- involve individuals at different levels in the charity and promote greater understanding of the charity's objectives and strategy.

4 ▼ Reserves policy

SORP 2000 requires trustees to include in their annual report a statement of the charity's policy on reserves, including the level of reserves held at the balance sheet date and why they are held. Trustees therefore need to consider the need for reserves in their charity and develop an appropriate policy and statement, which should be reviewed annually.

WHAT ARE RESERVES?

In this context, reserves are the unrestricted funds held as the general funds of the charity, often described as free reserves. In SORP 2000, the term 'reserves' is defined as follows:

> *In this SORP we use the term 'reserves' (unless otherwise indicated) to describe that part of a charity's income funds that is freely available for its general purposes. 'Reserves' are therefore the resources the charity has or can make available to spend for any or all of the charity's purposes once it has met its commitments and covered its other planned expenditure.*

SORP 2000 Appendix 1 Glossary

Designated funds are omitted when considering the charity's reserves. This will only apply to funds that are properly designated for a defined purpose, which should be explained in the notes to the accounts. Charity Commission guidance in CC19 (April 2002 edition) makes it clear that charities may not designate funds in order to present their levels of reserves as lower than they really are.

> *We expect charities to follow this recommendation and to ensure that the amount of any funds held as designated funds is appropriate to the purpose or use for which the funds have been designated. A charity will not be justified in creating, or transferring resources to a designated fund, where the main purpose of doing that is to allow the charity to show a reduced level of reserves.*

CC19 – Charities' Reserves

Trustees are under a duty to balance the needs of current and future beneficiaries of the charity. A charity needs to have sufficient reserves to allow it to cover known liabilities and contingencies, absorb setbacks and take advantage of change and opportunity. However, charities holding reserves that are greater than their needs will be subject to scrutiny and possible investigation by the Charity Commission.

RESERVES POLICY

The benefits of developing a reserves policy:

◆ It is a key element of the strategic plan – without a clear idea of the reserves you need you may not be able to meet your commitments or start new activities.

◆ It feeds into the budgeting and decision-making process – the policy will act as a benchmark to ensure that you use your funds to good effect. Without this the danger is that if you have high reserves you make take on projects without detailed planning, and with low funds you may be forced to be reactive rather than plan constructively.

◆ It focuses the fundraising activities – the reserves policy will identify your level of need for funds and what they are needed for. This can be fed into the fundraising plans as it is often easier to fundraise for specific items or amounts.

◆ It is necessary for communication with those external to the charity – the reserves policy helps to demonstrate that the charity's money is being used to good effect. Funders, beneficiaries, members and the wider public are entitled to know this, and also to know that you have good reasons for maintaining or seeking a certain level of reserves.

There are a number of different approaches to developing a reserves policy. Andrew Hind has successfully summarised these, and the summary below is taken from his text on charity reserves. (*See Further Information.*) Hind sets out four different approaches:

◆ **Justifying the status quo**

In this approach to setting a reserves policy, the trustees look at the actual level of reserves (usually relatively high) and create a reserves policy to justify the actual amounts held.

◆ **The 'Armageddon' approach**

The trustees assume the worst will happen and calculate the level of reserves needed to fund the closure of the charity's activities, including redundancy pay and the full cost of leases and commitments that would crystallise.

◆ **The 'actuarial liability' approach**

The charity assesses its future expenditure commitments and actuarially computes the funds needed to generate sufficient income to cover its expenditure commitments, similar to an endowment fund.

◆ **The risk identification approach**

This approach is based on an understanding of the income streams and their risk profile, the degree of commitment to expenditure and the overall risk environment in which the charity operates.

The last approach is the one recommended by Hind and now most commonly adopted by charities. The steps to developing a reserves policy on this basis are described in more detail below.

REASONS FOR HOLDING RESERVES

There are a number of reasons why charities may hold reserves and these will depend on the type of activity undertaken by the charity and how it operates and funds its operations. In general, reasons why charities hold reserves can be summarised as follows:

◆ To fund working capital

◆ To fund unexpected expenditure, for example when projects overrun or unplanned events occur

◆ To fund shortfalls in income, when income does not reach expected levels.

A helpful way for charities to view reserves is to see them as the funds they will use to cover expenditure to 'buy some time' in the event of reduced income or changes in circumstances. A charity may foresee that there is a chance that funding from a particular source will be cut, and so it will need reserves to fund committed expenditure whilst searching for alternative funding. The judgement of how long the charity will need to find alternative funding will help determine the size of the reserve needed for this purpose. For example, the charity may assess that it would need six months to replace a major source of funding. The reserves level to cover this contingency would therefore need to be the equivalent of six months funding or expenditure.

STEPS IN DEVELOPING A RESERVES POLICY

There is no standard formula that you can apply to a charity's set of accounts in order to establish the correct level of reserves for it. In a publication produced for the NCVO, *Not Just for a Rainy Day?*, Shirley Gillingham and John Tame set out a detailed approach involving a review along these lines:

◆ Analysis of existing funds

◆ Review of future income streams with an assessment of their level of reliability

◆ Review of committed expenditure and the extent to which this is controllable

♦ An assessment of the risks facing the charity, which should identify the potential commitments and contingencies and assess the likelihood of these materialising.

Analysis of existing funds

It is important to be clear about what your starting point is, i.e. your current level of reserves. Review the balance sheet for the following:

♦ Ensure that all endowment and restricted funds have been identified.

♦ Ensure that all your designated funds can be justified and that there are no more to add.

♦ Identify any assets that cannot be readily converted into cash.

Whilst technically the reserves funding long-term assets, such as tangible fixed assets, may be unrestricted reserves, in reality these are not available for distribution. It may be appropriate to identify the funding for fixed assets separately to reach an estimate for the free reserves of the charity.

Illustration: Analysis of existing funds

Camberwick Community Hall – Balance sheet

Tangible fixed assets – property	£680,000
Investments	£20,000
Net current assets	£50,000
Net assets and total reserves	**£750,000**

This charity has been running for a number of years. With the building of a large number of new houses in the area, there has been a sudden influx of new residents. The charity has received an offer of new funding of £0.75 million to fund expansion.

In the early years of the hall's life, maintenance costs were low. However, the caretaker has noticed that repair costs are creeping up and £10,000 was spent this year. The windows will need to be replaced in the next couple of years. A member of the committee who is also a local builder thinks these are likely to cost in the region of £50,000.

The management committee is concerned about the condition of the hall and the growing demands of the new members. The management committee needs to establish a reserves policy, which will explain to the members how their reserves are tied up in the property and how increasing repair costs can be met.

Analysis of the existing funds reveals that three designated funds should be set up:

♦ Tangible fixed assets fund – this will equal the net book value of the property.

♦ Cyclical maintenance fund – this will cover annual repair costs – suggested balance £10,000. This has been based on the costs incurred in 2002/03 and were thought to be the average annual cost of repairs. Costs will be charged against this fund and transfers added to the fund to cover future costs.

♦ Windows fund – this will be set up with a balance of £25,000 and will be added to in 2003/2004 so the costs of replacement windows can be covered in a couple of years' time when the work needs to be done.

The charity is left with £35,000 of free reserves, i.e. unrestricted, undesignated funds.

Camberwick Community Hall – Balance Sheet

Tangible fixed assets – property	£680,000
Investments	£20,000
Net current assets	£50,000
Net assets	**£750,000**
General reserves	£35,000
Designated funds:	
Tangible fixed asset fund	£680,000
Cyclical maintenance fund	£10,000
Windows fund	£25,000
Total funds	**£750,000**

Showing £35,000 as the general reserves gives a more accurate picture of the charity's financial position. Investments and current assets amount to £70,000, of which half will be needed for repairs to the building.

Review of future income streams

This review may also need to start with the current position. You start by looking at existing funding, with some assessment of the likelihood of the source of funding continuing. For example, a grant may be certain as it may be a multi-year award. For some organisations, membership subscriptions will be a stable source of income, although some allowance may have to be made for non-renewals.

Other risk factors should also be taken into account in assessing the funding sources. An income stream is more at risk if it comes from only one source, such as a major grant. A large number of small donations may have a lower risk profile because the chance that all donors will cease donating is very low. There is a high risk that a few donors will cease donating, but the financial impact is small. This can be taken into account when reviewing future income streams.

In addition, the loss of income will have a greater impact on the organisation if the source of income forms a high proportion of the overall income to the organisation.

A risk profile of future income streams can be built using the following information:

a) Type of income/source of funding

b) Current level in £

c) Proportion of total income as %

d) Do you expect the income level to go up or down? Rank as follows:

1 = steady increase – by 10% or more

2 = rapid increase – by 25% or more

3 = static

4 = decline

e) How many different people give under this form of funding, i.e. is this a single grant funder or many individuals? Rank as follows:

1 = very many

2 = several

3 = few

4 = one source or funder

f) How certain is the source of income for the future? Rank as follows:

1 = committed for indefinite future

2 = for a fixed period

3 = planning well underway or by implication – e.g. past pattern, verbal assurance

4 = not certain at all

You can multiply out the scores in the categories c) to f) to come to a number that will give the relative reliability of each type of income. Using the above ranking system means that a low score indicates a more reliable source of income. A high score means that there is greater risk attached to the source of income for a combination of reasons.

Using this system to rank each source or type of funding can help the organisation to produce a table to see the relative reliability of each source of funding and how secure their future income streams are. Clearly a charity with secure income streams has less need of reserves, whereas a charity with insecure future income needs higher levels of reserves.

Illustration: Review of future income streams

Access for All is a relatively new charity. Its recent accounts showed the following information:

	Restricted £'000	Unrestricted £'000	Total £'000
Incoming resources			
Government grants	74	-	74
Donations	716	692	1,408
Activities to generate funds			
Marathons	-	1,372	1,372
Overseas events	-	1,350	1,350
Other events	-	228	228
Investment income and interest	25	20	45
Total incoming resources	815	3,662	4,477

Resources expended

Cost of generating funds:

Marathons	-	415	**415**
Overseas events	-	480	**480**
Other events	-	37	**37**

Additional information about donations has been extracted as follows:

	Restricted £'000	Unrestricted £'000	Total £'000
Individuals	33	256	289
Corporate donations	279	418	697
Trusts	404	18	422
Total donations	**716**	**692**	**1,408**

Before we start ranking the reliability of income, there are two important aspects to take into account:

◆ Restricted income should be treated differently to unrestricted income. We can exclude restricted income from these calculations and exclude the related expenditure as well. This is consistent and is appropriate in this case where the proportion of restricted income is low. Alternatively, where the level of restricted income is high and it funds activities that are a core activity for the charity, then it is more appropriate to keep the restricted income in the reckoning for reliability of income. The related expenditure will then need to be included as well, as a firm commitment, in order to represent the status of that income and expenditure accurately.

◆ Some of the income relates to events and other activities that generate funds. In reality, the income to the charity from fundraising activity is the income less the related expenditure, so for this exercise, we need to include only the net income in our assessment of reliability.

So illustrated below is the assessment of unrestricted income for this charity, with fundraising income shown as the net income from activities.

	£'000	Proportion of income %	Likely change	Number of sources	Certainty	Reliability Score
Donations from individuals	256	9.38	1	1	3	28
Corporate donations	418	15.31	1	2	2	61
Trust donations	18	0.66	1	2	2	3
Marathons	957	35.05	3	1	3	315
Overseas events	870	31.87	4	1	3	382
Other events	191	7.00	3	1	3	63
Investment income	20	0.73	3	3	3	20
Total income net of direct costs	**2730**					

The overseas events and then the marathons have the highest score, by a significant margin. This reflects the high risk nature of such fundraising methods. Unfortunately for this charity, these events also produce the highest proportion of their income. As well as informing the strategic plan for the charity, this analysis will help the charity to develop their policy on reserves. They do not have very reliable income and need to consider how they will cover committed expenditure.

Review of committed expenditure

The next step in developing a reserves policy involves looking at the expenditure patterns and the extent to which the charity can curtail or change the timing of cash outflows. Ideally, an organisation should be timing cash outflows to match the timing of cash inflows. Where this is not possible, reserves may be needed to fund expenditure in advance of income receipts, or expenditure delayed.

You can build up a profile of the organisation's commitments using the following analysis:

a) Type of expenditure

b) Current level in £

c) Proportion of total expenditure as %

d) How significant is that type of expenditure to the charity's operations? How much does it contribute to the achievement of the charity's objects? Rank as follows:

    1 = unnecessary

    2 = optional

    3 = essential

    4 = core purpose

e) Consider the number of people affected by a decision to cut the expenditure, including beneficiaries and volunteers, as well as staff. Rank as follows:

    1 = one

    2 = few

    3 = several

    4 = very many

f) Identify the source of funding and score as follows:

    1 = general funding

    2 = grant

    3 = restricted income

    4 = contract

Multiply all the scores in c) to f) to produce a number. This is the commitment score. Based on the above system of scoring, higher scores indicate a greater degree of commitment to the expenditure line.

You can decide how to split up the expenditure, but a balance needs to be achieved between too much detail and insufficient detail. The purpose of this exercise is not to identify the types of expenditure which will be cut first, but to help to quantify the amount that may be needed in reserves to fund expenditure patterns.

Illustration: Review of committed expenditure

Support for Disabled Children makes grants to children and their families to fund the purchase of specialist equipment, and provides information and support to families. They raise a significant amount of funding from their own efforts, such as running lotteries and other fundraising activities. They generate restricted donations to fund much of the grants payable. An analysis of the accounts for the last financial year produces the following summary relating to expenditure:

Salaries including National Insurance	£392,708
Grants payable	£238,580
Direct costs of fundraising	£248,275
Office and general running costs	£171,296
Total expenditure	**£1,050,859**

	£'000	Proportion of expenditure %	Operational significance	Number of people affected	Source of funding	Commitment score
Salaries including National Insurance	393	37.37	2	4	1	298.96
Grants payable	239	22.70	4	4	3	1089.76
Direct costs of fundraising	248	23.63	1	2	1	47.25
Office and general running costs	171	16.30	3	3	1	146.71

Because grants are a core activity and they receive restricted funding for this activity, this will be the most difficult expenditure to curtail. Obviously salaries are always a major commitment, although within the salaries total there may be some temporary and project staff, which may be more controllable than staff engaged on core activities. This area may need further analysis.

Risk assessment

Consideration has already been given to some aspects of risk when reviewing the future income streams. This step in developing a reserves policy needs to consider other points that may have arisen when the charity reviewed the major risks to which the charity is exposed. In terms of the reserves policy, we are most concerned here with risks that represent a contingent liability or may crystallise into a commitment.

DRAWING THE POLICY UP

Having considered the reliability of income and the extent to which expenditure is committed, as well as the major risks to which the charity is exposed, the trustees will have gathered a significant amount of information on which to base the policy for their charity. They should now understand the reasons why their particular charity needs to hold reserves, rather than the more general reasons that apply to almost every undertaking. They can then consider the range of reserves levels that would be appropriate for the charity.

WHAT SHOULD THE POLICY CONTAIN?

As a minimum the policy should cover:

- ◆ the reasons why the charity needs reserves
- ◆ what level or range of reserves the trustees believe the charity needs
- ◆ what steps the charity is going to take to establish this agreed level or range
- ◆ arrangements for monitoring and reviewing the policy.

The charity's annual report needs to include a statement of the charity's policy on reserves, stating the level of reserves held and why they are held. The detailed policy developed following the steps described above can be summarised in a brief statement for the annual report.

Example: Reserves policy statement

Total reserves: £51.2 million

Reserves enable us to make long-term commitments to projects and also protect us against financial and economic downturns.

Unrestricted funds (£17 million) provide working capital to finance day-to-day activities.

Restricted funds (£14 million) are earmarked for particular projects and are carried over for spending in the next financial year.

The base reserve (£10 million) is our basic safety net against dramatic long-term swings in income or costs.

The fixed asset reserve (£5.4 million) represents the value of buildings and other assets in the UK.

Endowment funds (£2.8 million) are donations given by individuals on the condition that they are invested and the interest used to benefit children for years to come.

The emergency response reserve (£2 million) allows us to respond to emergencies immediately, before a fundraising appeal is launched.

Source: Save the Children Annual Report 2000/01

---

5 ▼ Investments

INVESTMENT POLICY

One of the key new requirements in the trustees' annual report under SORP 2000 is a statement of the charity's investment policy and performance against that policy.

Trustees have a duty to maximise the value of assets and therefore to invest them to obtain a good return. They also need to balance the needs of current and future beneficiaries. Trustees must exercise a duty of care over the way they manage investments. This goes beyond the normal duty of care expected from directors of a for-profit company as the trustees are acting in a stewardship role. This aspect of the trustees' responsibilities for investment is explored at various points in this chapter.

The investment policy must be compatible with the reserves policy, and it is logical to work on the reserves policy before the investment policy. Once there is a clear target level of reserves for the charity, together with income, expenditure and cashflow projections for a number of years, it is possible to establish the level of funds available to invest, together with target returns for income and capital growth.

The work carried out by the charity looking at key risks will also impact on the investment policy. As well as the obvious risk of lost income if assets are inappropriately invested, there are other non-financial risks. For example, a cancer charity holding tobacco stocks within an investment portfolio risks its reputation and good name.

The investment policy needs to include:

- type of investment;
- target return;
- risk profile;
- ethical considerations;
- any specific legal powers or restrictions.

An investment policy should be reviewed at least annually. It should be updated to take account of both the changing needs of the charity and changes to the external environment.

The following factors should be taken into account when drawing up an investment policy.

Powers to invest

The Trustee Act 2000 came into force on 1 February 2001 and applies to all charities set up as trusts or unincorporated charities, but not to charitable companies. The act sets out a new general power of investment, which allows a trustee to place funds in any kind of investment, excluding land, as though he or she is the owner of those funds. There is also now a separate power to acquire land as an investment.

If the governing document restricts powers of investment, then this restriction or exclusion will still apply. This must be taken into account when drawing up a policy, and is required under the SORP to be disclosed in the trustees' annual report.

The investment powers for charitable companies will be set out in their memorandum and articles of association.

For charities now covered by the Trustee Act 2000, this new general power of investment is wider than that previously allowed (under the Trustee Investments Act 1961). You will need to ensure that the existing portfolio is appropriate, given these wider powers.

Risk profile

Trustees need to invest in order to obtain a good return. However, they should not risk losing assets by, for example, investing in a highly speculative venture. They must therefore balance risk with return. Trustees need to agree on an acceptable risk profile for their investment portfolio, taking into consideration the objectives of their investment policy.

Care needs to be taken here and advice can be sought from your investment manager (if one has been appointed). For example, cash deposits are often perceived to be low risk, but over a longer term period, inflation is likely to undermine the real value of these holdings.

One key method to reduce risk is to ensure that the charity's portfolio is sufficiently well diversified. The need for diversification is laid out in the Trustee Act 2000. The Charity Commission frequently asks questions where they find that a charity has a poorly diversified portfolio. As well as covering the allocation of funds between different types of assets, the need to diversify applies to the stock holdings within a particular asset type.

Types of investments

When drawing up a policy, you will need to consider the types of investments you are willing to invest in. This will depend upon how long the investment can be held, the agreed risk profile and the required rate of return.

The types of investments available range from cash deposit accounts and Common Deposit Funds, through gilts, such as government stocks, to equities, whether pooled within Common Investment Funds and unit trusts, or individual holdings. Land and property may also be considered. Derivatives, such as futures and options, are highly speculative and not generally considered suitable for charities.

Total return

A total return approach to investing aims to maximise the overall investment return, rather than specifying the amount expected in the form of income and in the form of capital gain. The capital gains, dividends and interest income are pooled.

Charities with a permanent endowment historically have had to allocate capital returns to the capital fund and income returns to the income fund. Given that the capital fund cannot be spent, this has not always resulted in the needs of present and future beneficiaries being treated evenly.

In May 2001, the Charity Commission produced new operational guidance. This gives trustees of permanently endowed charities the right to apply for permission to adopt a policy of total return. This will give them the flexibility to allocate an appropriate part of investment return to the distributable income funds of the charity.

If an endowed charity has obtained such permission, then this needs to be disclosed in the trustees' annual report. The charity also needs to disclose the date from which this is applied and the value of the unspent investment return at that date. Also, trustees need to explain the considerations and policies relevant to their decision on how much total return to apply to income in that year. Finally, given that the trustees are required to obtain proper advice in this respect, they need to identify the investment adviser or other person(s) giving this advice.

Benchmarking

To be able to effectively monitor the success of an investment policy, you need to set targets for performance and monitor that performance against these targets. It will probably be appropriate to set a benchmark against which performance is measured. This may be one of the standard measures published by the WM Charity Service. If this is not appropriate, perhaps due to constraints over the charity's investments, then a specific benchmark can be agreed (usually through discussions with your fund manager). (*See Further Information* for details of benchmarking services.)

The trustees' annual report will then disclose the agreed targets and the actual results compared with these targets, and will seek to offer an explanation for the subsequent variances. The key here is to demonstrate that the trustees were acting in the best interests of the charity, taking account of risk, return and other issues as discussed above.

Ethical and socially responsible investment

Charities are increasingly taking account of ethical issues when setting investment policies. There are, however, legal issues to consider before adopting a wide-ranging ethical policy. A crucial court case in 1991 brought by the Bishop of Oxford against the Church Commissioners established that the trustees must hold the interests of the beneficiaries paramount and that this generally meant that the return on investments should be maximised as a priority. Subsequent Charity Commission guidance has confirmed this. However, it is acceptable to avoid investments that directly contravene the charity's objects and purposes. Beyond that, trustees need to consider the overall return on investments and the requirement to maximise return. Trustees may also take into account the potential damage to the charity through poor publicity should donors and supporters not support the investment policy. For example, an investment policy that avoids companies that damage the environment may be seen as essential for an environmental charity wishing to retain the support of donors and members.

If you adopt a policy of ethical investment, you need to explain the constraints you have applied within the investment policy in the trustees' annual report.

Charities that choose to adopt an ethical policy need to be able to obtain sufficient information on their proposed investments to ensure that their actual investments are in compliance with the policy. In 1983, a group of churches and charities that had investments and strong convictions of what they considered ethical helped to set up EIRIS. EIRIS is a charity that provides independent research into the social, environmental and ethical performance of companies. It can provide charities with the information they need to put their own principles into practice when making investment decisions. (*See Further Information.*)

As well as investing ethically, there is now interest amongst charities in socially responsible or programme-related investment. This is where charities can invest in ways that meet their charitable objects, rather than simply investing to maximise returns and then using the returns to help the charity's beneficiaries. While a programme-related investment has both financial and social objectives, the charity's sole aim is to help its beneficiaries in accordance with its charitable purposes. If handled well, programme-related investments can significantly increase the help a charity can offer in the short term, while not affecting the charity's longer term future. In their recent guidance, the Charity Commission has stated that a programme-related investment is not an 'investment' in the conventional sense of a financial investment, as it is also an application of funds in furtherance of charitable objects. Therefore, the normal strict rules on financial investments, for example in the Trustee Act 2000, do not apply.

Charities considering programme-related investments need to ensure that they have the necessary powers. They will also need to weigh up the risks and rewards of this type of investment carefully and consider how this activity will help the charity to meet its objectives. The justification for this investment should be fully explained in the trustees' annual report. Programme-related investments use the charity's income, sometimes in combination with the charity's endowment, and may take the form of a grant, a loan or the purchase of shares. The accounting treatment should reflect the type of transaction.

Investment managers

Under the Trustee Act 2000, trustees have a power to employ agents to manage the charity's investments and to appoint nominees or custodians of the charity's assets. There should be a written agreement with such agents and their performance should be kept under review.

The trustees' annual report should state whether agents have been appointed and demonstrate that the investment managers are implementing the agreed policy and reporting regularly to the trustees.

Example: Investment policy

The Rosanna Grant Trust

There are no restrictions on the charity's power to invest. The investment strategy is set by the trustees for a period of five years and takes account of recent demands for funds and the quality of the funding applications. The trustees consider the income requirements, the risk profile and the investment managers' view of the market prospects in the medium term. This strategy is set within an overall policy that states that the endowment fund is to be invested in low- and medium-risk investments with a view to ensuring that capital appreciation of the fund exceeds inflation over each five-year period. The unrestricted and restricted reserves may be invested in any type of investment. Our strategy is reviewed with our investment managers annually. In the year, the charity estimated that it required income of £780,000 and implemented a low-risk strategy. Income fell short of the target by £50,000.

Source: Source: CC66 SORP 2000 Example Reports and Accounts

The Rosanna Grant Trust is an example of an unincorporated endowed organisation that has chosen not to adopt a total return strategy for the management of its investments. The example clearly explains the process that has taken place in drawing up an investment policy, particularly focusing on the funds available to invest. It also explains the risk strategy adopted and the types of investments included. It sets a target and compares performance to that target.

Example: Investment policy

The ABC Charity

The charity has adopted a total returns policy for its investment income. The investment managers work towards a target return agreed with the trustees. During the year the return on stock market investments was eight per cent. Although this was below the target return of nine per cent, the charity's investment managers have exceeded the target over the last three years. As permitted by the charity's memorandum and articles of association, the trustees have given the investment managers discretion to manage the portfolio within an agreed risk profile. It is the charity's policy to specifically exclude investments in the armaments sector.

Source: Source: CC66 SORP 2000 Example Reports and Accounts

The ABC Charity is a charitable company. There is no permanent endowment, so it has no need to obtain consent to adopt a total return strategy. This example again demonstrates performance against target and outlines the delegation of management to the investment managers' discretion. There is a specific ethical restriction on investments here.

Example: Investment policy

Aid Overseas

The trustees have the power to invest in such assets as they see fit.

The charity sometimes needs to react very quickly to particular emergencies and has a policy of keeping any surplus liquid funds in short-term deposits that can be accessed readily. The charity has an active treasury management department and is pleased to report that it has obtained a return of six per cent on interest on these deposits. The charity has some investment property that it acquired by virtue of vacating one of its premises and letting the remainder of the space to an existing tenant. It is not our policy to hold such properties and therefore we plan to sell the freehold in the forthcoming financial year.

Source: CC66 SORP 2000 Example Reports and Accounts

Aid Overseas gives an example of a service-providing charity that has made a decision to hold investments in cash deposits. The rationale for this is clearly explained and, as required, the charity still has a proper investment policy that is regularly monitored.

Example: Ethical investment policies

British Heart Foundation

The foundation's policy on investments and the tobacco industry has continued unchanged for over a decade. The foundation does not, and would not knowingly, hold in its investment portfolio shares in the tobacco industry. No shares are acquired in an investment or unit trust that has an identifiable holding in tobacco shares. If, subsequent to the foundation making an investment, the foundation discovers that an investment or unit trust has acquired tobacco stock, then the holding in that trust will be sold as soon as practicable.

Source: British Heart Foundation Annual Report and Accounts 2000

Example: Ethical Investment Policies

Barnardo's

The council has formulated an ethical investment policy that seeks to avoid investing in companies whose activities are considered to be to the detriment of children. Barnardo's retains the services of Ethical Investment Research Services (EIRIS) to advise on ethical investment issues.

Source: Barnardo's Annual Report and Accounts 2000

ACCOUNTING FOR INVESTMENTS

The general principle introduced under the 1995 SORP is that investments are revalued to market value at the balance sheet date and this has been retained in SORP 2000. This states that investments should be categorised separately within the fixed assets of the charity on the balance sheet, unless the intention is to realise them without reinvestment of the sales proceeds; in this case, they should be reclassified as a current asset.

Revaluation to market value will result in a gain or loss that will be reported in the revaluation section of the SoFA. The gain or loss is unrealised when this relates to a movement in the market value for shares still held at the end of the financial year.

A realised gain will be calculated by reference to the market value of the investments at the beginning of the financial year. For investments bought and sold in the same financial year, then the calculation is by reference to purchase price (cost).

Unrealised gains and losses

	For new investments		For investments retained all year
	Market value at end of the financial year		Market value at end of the financial year
less:	Cost when purchased	less:	Market value at the beginning of the year
equals:	Unrealised gain or loss	equals:	Unrealised gain or loss

Realised gains and losses

	For new investments		For investments held at beginning of year
	Sales proceeds		Sales proceeds
less:	Cost when purchased	less:	Market value at the beginning of the year
equals:	Realised gain or loss	equals:	Realised gain or loss

Illustration: Calculation of realised and unrealised gains

A charity had an investment portfolio valued at £345,000 as of 1 April 2000. During the year the following transactions took place:

- Shares worth £86,000 on 1 April 2000 were sold for £78,000 on 31 August 2000.
- £72,000 of these proceeds were reinvested in unit trusts (worth £70,500 at 31 March 2001).
- £52,500 worth of shares purchased on 10 April 2000 were then sold for £94,000 on 20 December 2000.
- The remaining portfolio was valued at £376,000 on 31 March 2001.

The realised gain/loss is calculated as follows:
Gain/loss on investments held at start of year and sold during year

i.e. £78,000 – £86,000 = £(8,000)

plus

Gain/loss on any investments purchased and sold within the year

i.e. £94,000 – £52,500 = £41,500

The total realised gain is therefore £33,500.

The unrealised gain/loss is calculated as follows:
Gain/loss on investments purchased during the year

i.e. market value at year-end less cost of investments purchased in year

£70,500 – £72,000 = £(1,500)

plus

Gain or loss on investments held throughout the year

i.e. market value at year-end less market value at start of year (book value brought forward) for investments held all year

(£376,000 – £70,500 [this gives you the year-end market value for investments held all year]) – (£345,000 – £86,000 [this gives you the opening market value of the investments that are not sold during the year]) = £46,500

The total unrealised gain is therefore £45,000 (£46,500 – £1,500).

For unincorporated charities, a change to the requirements under SORP 2000 means that realised and unrealised gains and losses may now be combined in a single line. In the example, therefore, only a total gain of £78,500 would need to be disclosed.

For charitable companies, however, there is still a Companies Act requirement to show these unrealised and realised gains and losses separately. This is because a company income and expenditure account must not include unrealised losses. The layout of the SoFA can be adapted to produce the income and expenditure account required for companies and then continue with the further information required by the SORP. A subheading 'Net income/expenditure for the year' should be inserted after the line for realised gains/losses and before the line for unrealised gains/losses.

Extract from SoFA – after total resources expended
Net incoming resources for the year
Realised gains on investment assets (analysis only required in charitable companies)
Net income/expenditure for the year (needed to comply with Companies Act)
Unrealised gains on investment assets
Net movement in funds
Funds brought forward
Funds carried forward

NOTES TO THE ACCOUNTS

Further information concerning investments is required in the notes to the accounts by SORP 2000.

Accounting policy

The policy for including investments in the accounts should be stated. This should be market value, but may need to be modified for valuation of unlisted investments, investment properties and other investments that do not have a readily quoted value.

There should also be an accounting policy to describe the basis of inclusion in the SoFA of unrealised and realised gains and losses.

Note on investments

All changes in value of investment assets and movements on investments should be described, reconciling opening and closing book values shown in the balance sheets for the two years in the accounts.

	£
Opening book value/market value brought forward	X
Additions in year (at cost)	X
Disposals in year (at opening book value)	(X)
(being sales proceeds plus realised loss or less realised gain)	
Unrealised gain/loss on revaluation	X
Closing book value/market value carried forward	X

In addition, the notes need to show the historic cost of investments at the beginning of the financial year (brought forward) and at the end of the financial year (carried forward).

Illustration: Accounting note showing changes in value of investment assets for a charitable company

Quoted investments	£
Market value at beginning of year	345,000
Less: Disposals at opening book value (proceeds £172,000; gain £33,500)	(138,500)
Add: Acquisitions at cost	124,500
Net unrealised gain on revaluation at end of year	45,000
Market value at end of year	**376,000**

Because this is for a charitable company, the unrealised gain (£45,000) and the realised gain (£33,500) have been split, as they will need to be on the face of the SoFA to comply with the Companies Act.

For unincorporated charities, disposals can be included as the total amount of the sales proceeds plus or minus the total gain or loss.

Illustration: Accounting note showing changes in value of investment assets for an unincorporated charity:

Quoted investments	£
Market value at beginning of the year	345,000
Less: Disposals	(172,000)
Add: Acquisitions	124,500
Net gain on revaluation at end of the year	78,500
Market value at end of the year	**376,000**

For an unincorporated charity, the split of realised and unrealised gains is unnecessary. Disposals are therefore included at proceed value, and the total combined gain of £78,500 shown.

Types of investments

Total value divided between distinct types:

+ Investment properties
+ listed investments, including unit trusts and common investment funds
+ Investments in subsidiary or associated undertakings
+ Other unlisted securities
+ Cash held as part of portfolio
+ Any other investments.

Each of these should be further subdivided into investments held in the UK and those held outside the UK.

The note should give details of any material investments. Material means that the holding is more than five per cent by value of the total investment portfolio. From this, readers of the accounts, including the Charity Commission, will be able to see whether a portfolio is sufficiently diversified. Also, significant investment holdings will be publicly visible, which may have an impact for public relations if the investment is not seen as compatible with the charity's objects.

The note should also disclose any material restrictions that might apply on realisation of any such assets.

Example: Note showing analysis of investments

	2000		1999	
	Market value £'000	Cost £'000	Market value £'000	Cost £'000
Listed investments				
United Kingdom	104,934	87,827	120,417	89,927
Overseas	14,006	13,543	2,047	2,223
Subtotal: Listed investments	118,940	101,370	122,464	92,150
Unit trusts	42,210	35,679	60,314	40,914
Unlisted investments	4	19	4	19
Cash deposits	5,155	5,155	3,717	3,717
Investment in subsidiaries	481	504	494	504
Total of all investments	**166,790**	**142,727**	**186,993**	**137,304**

The market value of listed investments is the mid-market price quoted on a recognised stock exchange, the value of unit trusts is the mid-bid and offer price of the units, and the value of the unlisted investments is as determined by the council, all as at close of business at the year-end.
Included in unit trusts are two holdings representing more than five per cent of the total value of the investments, one a holding of £17.5m in the Merrill Lynch 33KWS – Overseas Fund, and the other amounting to £10.8 m in Charinco.

Source: The Guide Dogs for the Blind Association Report & Financial Statements 2000

Value of investments held in each type of fund of the charity

A note should show how the investments relate to the funds of the charity. This can be included within another note analysing net assets between charity funds.

Total return

If an endowed charity has decided to adopt a total return strategy (*see earlier in chapter*), there needs to be a note reconciling the total return for the year to the unapplied total return when the policy was first adopted, and showing how much has been applied in the year.

Balance sheet disclosure

Where fixed asset investments are revalued upwards, the difference between the original net book value and the new revalued amount is a revaluation reserve. Charitable companies need to disclose this reserve separately on the face of the balance sheet – this should be a subheading under the relevant fund in the funds section.

SoFA information

Investment management costs should be included within 'Cost of generating funds' on the SoFA. They should be shown as a separate category within this if material (on face of SoFA or in note).

PRACTICAL ASPECTS

Assessing available funds to invest

Before developing an investment policy and implementing it, the trustees need to establish how much they have available to invest. It is helpful to break down the funding requirements in terms of:

♦ money that is needed immediately as working capital to run the charity. This needs to be accessible at short notice. However, there is still scope for effective treasury management; for example, through the use of overnight cash deposits with the bank;

♦ money that can be committed for up to a month or longer. This is money that is not needed for day-to-day expenses but may need to be accessed for known liabilities in the medium term or, for example, due to changes in funding arrangements. Again, term deposits are available through the banking system on one to three months' notice to give this flexibility;

♦ money that can be committed for the longer term. Having identified the money needed for the immediate and medium term, you will be able to see how much is available for longer term investment. Longer term funds can then be invested into Common Investment Funds, or made up into a portfolio with a fund manager. Generally, investment managers advise that funds should be available to invest for five years or more for a proper investment strategy to be established. It is also important that you should not have to sell equities unexpectedly, as you may not obtain the best price.

In order to reach conclusions on the funds available, trustees need to consider the following:

- Reserves policy – Clearly much of the work that has produced the reserves policy will be relevant here. For example, a charity may have decided that reserves of nine months' running costs are appropriate. This could then be broken down between reserves required at short notice (say three or four months), and reserves for which longer notice can be given (say five or six months).

- Cashflow forecasts – Irrespective of the level of funds, all charities should produce a detailed cashflow projection to allow effective treasury management. The cashflow forecast will be based on information in the budget but will take account of the actual timings of cash receipts and payments. It will also consider capital purchases as opposed to depreciation. It is effectively predicting the available cash in the future. Ideally this should be prepared on a monthly basis and should look forward at least 12 months. It may also be necessary to predict further ahead if establishing available funds for investment in a fund-managed portfolio.

Accounting for investments during the year

The examples given earlier in this chapter showing the calculation of realised and unrealised gains and losses were for only four transactions in the year. Clearly it would not be so easy to calculate these gains and losses at the year-end for a large share portfolio. A system needs to be put in place, therefore, to monitor the investment transactions during the year and produce the required information for the accounts.

Investment managers tend to produce reports on a quarterly basis, detailing the market value at the end of each quarter and the transactions during the quarter (sales, purchases and capital reorganisations). These reports do not give the realised gains or losses on sales, since this is a unique concept to charity accounts. They give the proceeds and the profits over initial cost.

The simplest way to monitor investment movements for a large portfolio is to keep a register of investments. This can be maintained on a spreadsheet and updated on receipt of the report each quarter.

This will show:

- stock name
- holding quantity brought forward
- book value brought forward
- cost for purchases

- quantity of purchases
- proceeds for sales
- quantity for sales
- book value brought forward for sales
- realised gain or loss
- quantity carried forward
- book value carried forward
- market value carried forward
- unrealised gain or loss.

If this is regularly updated each quarter then you will easily be able to produce the calculations and other information required for the statutory accounts.

Investment properties

An investment property is a property that a charity holds as an investment, the disposal of which would not have a significant effect on any operations of the organisation. This means that the property is held primarily for the purpose of producing income for the charity. This is demonstrated by any rental income being negotiated at an arm's length basis. A property that is owned and occupied by a charity, or that of a subsidiary company, for its own purposes is not therefore classed as an investment property.

Accounting treatment for investment properties

Investment properties should be included on the balance sheet at open market value. The valuation does not have to be made by a qualified or independent valuer. However, the financial statements must disclose the names or qualifications of the valuers, the basis used by them, and whether the person making the valuation is an employee or officer of the company.

Valuations must be done at least every five years. In the meanwhile, the trustees must obtain advice as to the possibility of any material movements between individual valuations. If there is a material movement, the investment properties must be revalued.

Investment properties should not be depreciated. Any changes in value during the year, whether or not realised, should be reported in the 'gains and losses on revaluations and disposals of investment assets' section of the SoFA.

6 ▼ Grantmaking

Where grantmaking is a 'material' part of the charity's activities, the SORP requires charities to include their grant-making policies and an analysis of grants made in their annual report and accounts.

WHAT IS A GRANT?

According to the SORP, a grant is any payment which, in order to further its objects, a charity makes voluntarily to another institution or an individual. However, a payment that a charity must make in return for the supply of goods or services is not a grant.

WHEN IS GRANTMAKING MATERIAL TO A CHARITY?

Whether or not grantmaking is material to a charity depends on the size of the charity and the importance of grantmaking to its overall operation. The SORP criterion is that, if in any accounting year a charity makes grants totalling at least five per cent of its total resources expended in that year, then the charity should regard its grantmaking as material.

There may be other situations where the provision of further information on grants made could be considered necessary or desirable. For example, a charity may choose to give the bulk of its grants to just one organisation. Even if the amount does not constitute five per cent of the total resources expended in the year, this fact may be relevant as the grant will be very significant in terms of the total grants made. Disclosure of additional information beyond the minimum specified in the SORP is at the discretion of the trustees, with the over-riding requirement that sufficient information should be given to enable a reader of the report and accounts to gain an understanding of the charity's objects and how grantmaking fulfils them.

STATEMENT OF FINANCIAL ACTIVITIES

If grantmaking is material, the total amount of expenditure on grants payable in furtherance of the charity's objects needs to be disclosed separately on the face of the SoFA. This will be shown as part of the charitable expenditure.

TRUSTEES' ANNUAL REPORT

The SORP requires trustees to disclose any grant-making policies in the annual report. The minimum for a policy should be the criteria for grants and how decisions are reached on grantmaking. However, good practice suggests that the grant-making policy should include:

◆ the types of activities or organisations that will be funded

◆ any restrictions, such as geographical area, organisation type or activity that may be funded

◆ any levels set for grantmaking, including any breakdown, for example, by activity or area

◆ any restrictions on the amounts of individual grants

◆ the timeframe of grants, whether one-off or over a number of years

◆ the policy with regard to reapplication, if unsuccessful or if current funding is coming to an end

◆ how grants are assessed, which individuals, committees or sub-committees have decision-making power on grants

◆ how grants are monitored.

Example: Grant-making policy – The Rosanna Grant Trust

The charity invites applications for funding of projects through advertising in specialist medical media. Institutional applicants are invited to submit a summary of their proposals in a specific format. The applications are reviewed against specific criteria and research objectives which are set by the scientific panel. Most projects are funded for three years and are monitored on an annual basis.

The charity also invites individuals from any part of the world carrying out PhD or MD studies concerned with Alzheimer's Disease and related matters to apply for scholarships. These can amount to a maximum of £9,000 per annum. Applicants are asked to provide a summary of their proposed thesis and in certain cases are invited to interview by a scholarship panel. Progress towards a PhD is monitored every six months.

The charity requests a copy of the final reports on each piece of research which are made publicly available.

Source: CC66 SORP 2000 Example Reports and Accounts

Additional information

There are other areas that may not form part of the formal grant-making policy, but would provide readers with useful additional information and therefore may be included in the trustees' annual report.

Detailed assessment criteria

The trustees' annual report is a public document and it is likely that it will be studied by prospective grant applicants. It therefore presents an opportunity to clearly set out the assessment criteria. As grantmakers will be aware, a significant proportion of applications fail to meet even the initial selection criteria. This presents a considerable administrative burden, and it is therefore in everyone's interests for these criteria to be well-publicised to keep invalid applications to a minimum. There is also a growing demand for transparency and so this additional information helps to make the grantmaking process more transparent.

Current targets for grantmaking

Although not part of the formal policy, a charity may take a decision in a particular year to target a specific geographical location or group. This will need to be properly publicised to help to achieve this aim.

Links to other policies

The policy on grantmaking may be inherently linked to the reserves policy or investment policy of the charity. If this is the case, then any link will need to be explained. For example, a permanently endowed charity may be able to use only the income return on investment.

Designating funds

Some charities include future grants in designated funds (*see Accounting treatment below*) and this may warrant further explanation.

Example: Trustees' annual report – The Diana, Princess of Wales Memorial Fund

The trustees have set a medium-term annual average of at least £7 million for the award of grants, even if this were to mean drawing on the fund's capital.

The trustees are concentrating on a limited number of broad priority themes for the award of UK and international grants:

♦ Displaced people

♦ People at the margins of society

♦ Survivors of conflict and those requiring conflict mediation

♦ Dying and bereaved people.

The trustees have focused on particular areas of need for each year within these broad themes and will revise and adjust the criteria for funding from time to time. The intention is to make a limited number of substantial grants rather than a large number of small ones and to concentrate on groups and causes that would otherwise find it difficult to receive recognition and support.

Source: Annual Report and Accounts 2001 The Diana, Princess of Wales Memorial Fund

---

ANALYSIS OF GRANTS

The SORP requires an appropriate analysis and explanation of the grants made. This can be included in the notes to the accounts, as part of the trustees' annual report, or as a separate publication. The purpose of this analysis is 'to help the reader of the accounts understand how the grants made relate to the objects of the charity and the policy adopted by the trustees in pursuing these objects'. (Statement of Recommended Practice paragraph 140)

The analysis of grantmaking needs to distinguish institutional and individual grants. This information will usually be included in the notes to the accounts.

An individual grant is one that is made for the direct benefit of the individual who receives it (for example, to relieve financial hardship). Benevolent funds, for example, predominantly make grants to individuals.

All other grants are institutional grants. A grant to an individual to carry out a research project is therefore regarded as a grant to the institution with which the individual is connected, rather than as a grant to the individual.

The notes to the accounts should show the total number of individual and institutional grants, and the total value of grants given for different charitable purposes. The charity should decide upon classifications that are appropriate for an understanding of the policy. The example given in the SORP groups institutional grants into social welfare, medical research, and the performing arts. Individual grants are grouped, for example, into welfare of those in financial need or help, people seeking to further their education, and so on.

Illustration: Analysis of grants

As a result of the serious problem of AIDS in Africa, the trustees made a policy decision in 1997 to increase support to projects there. This is clearly demonstrated by the fact that the total expenditure on grants to Africa has increased by 46% in three years. This trend can also be seen from the breakdown of grants by region over the last three years:

	(percentage of total grants)		
	1999	2000	2001
South America	35	23	19
South East Asia	23	14	11
South Africa	5	11	14
Rest of Africa	37	52	56

The decision in the last financial year to focus on environmental and conservation issues has been rewarded by a threefold increase in successful applications in this area, as highlighted in the notes to the accounts. Total expenditure in these areas now, therefore, accounts for 52% of grant-making activity (2000 – 23%) and £1,452,000 (2000 – £578,000).

This is an opportunity for the grantmaker to further explain the work of the charity. If the detailed analysis is included in the notes to the accounts, then the trustees' annual report can be used to explain this further. For example, it can highlight particular trends or the effect of a particular policy decision by trustees.

The Wellcome Trust provides a detailed analysis in the notes to the financial statements. This analyses grants according to the scientific area

	2000 £m	1999 £m	2000 Number	1999 Number
Genetics	82.8	45.0	25	8
Molecular and cell biology	48.3	29.8	181	171
Infection and immunity	45.6	33.2	170	158
Neurosciences	32.1	43.9	174	196
Tropical medicine	27.8	11.2	87	96

Source: The Wellcome Trust Annual Report and Accounts 2000

In addition to this analysis, additional information should be given for institutional grants. For grants over £1,000, the name of the recipient institution and the number and total value of grants made to that institution in the accounting year should be provided. If more than 50 such grants have been made, the information should cover the largest 50 grants or any larger number that is necessary for a proper understanding of the charity's grantmaking. For fewer than 50 such grants, the information should be given for all of them.

Note that if grants have been made to a particular institution for different charitable purposes, the number and total value of grants made for each purpose should be given.

Both the analysis of grants grouped by category and the disclosure of grant institutions by name need to be reconciled to the total grant expenditure on the SoFA. It may therefore be necessary to list in total the grants to individuals and other smaller grants to institutions in order for this note to reconcile to the amount given for grants payable in the SoFA.

The example for a grant-making trust in CC66 shows the amount of information to be provided and appropriate ways in which to present it

Example: Analysis of grants payable

The Rosanna Grant Trust

The amount payable in the year comprises:

	2001 £'000	2001 £'000	2000 £'000	2000 £'000
Education and research				
Manchester Institute of Technology				
4 grants (2000 – 4 grants) as follows:				
To fund educational post	51		36	
Genetic research	31		31	
Research into awareness of symptoms of Alzheimer's in general practitioners	20		20	
The impact of Alzheimer's on family and carers	21		21	
		123		108
University of Slough				
2 grants to fund educational posts (2000 – 1 grant)		91		57
University of Taunton				
2 grants (2000 – 3 grants) as follows:				
Research into drug therapies	51		49	
Research on nursing homes caring for patients with Alzheimer's	34		30	
Compilation of registry of practitioners and hospitals specialising in Alzheimer's	-		24	
		85		103
		299		268
Total institutional grants				
PhD scholarships – grants to 79 individuals (2000 – 52 individuals)		244		153
		543		421

Source: CC66 SORP 2000 Example Reports and Accounts

Separate publication

It is possible to provide the analysis and explanation of grants payable in a separate publication, as an alternative to including this within the notes to the accounts or the trustees' annual report. If you choose this option, you need to explain this in the notes to the accounts and identify how copies can be obtained.

The SORP also explains when it is acceptable to omit the details of the recipient institution. This is where disclosure could seriously prejudice the furtherance of the purposes either of the recipient institution or of the charity itself. In these circumstances, a charity may withhold details of each grant concerned, but should:

- disclose in the notes to the accounts the total number, value and general purpose of those grants not included;

- before the trustees sign the accounts, give the full details of such grants in writing to the Charity Commission or other appropriate regulatory body, fully explaining the reasons why those details have not been included in the accounts;

- state in the trustees' annual report whether or not these details have been given to the regulatory body.

The SORP then states that it is unlikely that all the material institutional grants of a charity would fall within this exception.

ACCOUNTING TREATMENT

Historically, it has not always been clear to organisations at which point they should recognise a grant as a liability in the accounts. This has been clarified with the introduction of Financial Reporting Standards (FRSs) 5 and 12. These have been explained and incorporated into SORP 2000.

As soon as there is a liability committing the charity to expenditure, the grant expenditure should be recognised in the charity's accounts. This liability may arise as a result of a legal obligation or a constructive obligation. When a funder makes a grant, this is usually set out in an offer letter, and may be accompanied by conditions of grant funding. Typically, the wording of grant award letters and the terms of the conditions rarely mean that the grant constitutes a legally binding agreement. A grant award is therefore rarely a legal obligation, although this will depend on the terms.

A constructive obligation is a moral obligation where a valid expectation has been created in the mind of the recipient (or possibly a third party) that the grant will be paid. This could be as a result of past practice (promised grants have always been paid), published policies or a specific current statement (public pronouncement made by the charity or the wording of the grant offer, for example). So, even where there is no legal liability, there may be a liability in the accounts, due to the presence of a constructive obligation.

A grant will not be a liability if there are specific conditions that need to be met before that grant can be paid. This potential commitment will probably still need to be disclosed in the accounts as a contingent liability, but not included in expenditure.

Illustration: Accounting for grant commitments

A medical research charity makes grants to individuals based at universities for research. These grants are offered for a three-year period. However, a detailed review is required at the end of the first year's funding before a commitment to a second or third year is made. This review looks at the particular project in great detail, as it is possible to establish at that stage the value of the work to the charity. If it is recommended that the project be continued, the approval of

---

the third year of funding is considered by all to be a foregone conclusion. The charity would not be able to reasonably justify stopping a project so close to completion.

The expected treatment of such a grant in the accounts would be as follows.

- The first year's grant will be included in expenditure under grants payable as soon as it has been approved by the relevant committee.
- The second and third years' grants will not be included as expenditure at that time.
- As there is more than a remote possibility that the second and third years' grants will be paid, then this grant will be disclosed in the notes to the accounts as a contingent liability. All such second and third year grants could be grouped together. The contingent liability note should be phrased as follows: 'Although research projects are potentially supported for the full three years duration, only the first year's grant is included in expenditure. This is because a detailed review is carried out at the end of the first year, and future funding is dependent upon that. At this time, the second and third years' grants that are authorised but subject to this successful review total £433,000 (2000 – £389,000).'
- The trustees may choose to designate the total £433,000 potential commitment in the accounts, although there is no requirement to do this.
- There is a high probability of a third year's funding being awarded, once the second year's has been approved. In this situation, therefore, the third year's grant should be accrued in the accounts once the second year's funding has been approved.
- The SORP suggests that it may be necessary to reduce future payments to take account of their value at today's terms. In this case, the timescale is short and the grant accrued will be paid out the following year, so this is unnecessary.

NOTES TO THE ACCOUNTS

The information to be disclosed in the notes to the accounts with regard to the accounting treatment includes the relevant accounting policies and other details:

- The accounting policy explaining at what point grants are recognised as both expenditure and an accrual in the accounts. For example, when the grants committee makes a decision, or when conditions are fulfilled.
- The movement on any designated fund and an explanation of the purpose of that fund.
- Details regarding any contingent liabilities (which can be grouped together if similar), explaining the nature of the uncertainty and the financial effect.

Example: Accounting policy

The Rosanna Trust

Grants payable are charged in the year when the offer is conveyed to the recipient except in those cases where the offer is conditional, such grants being recognised as expenditure when the conditions attached are fulfilled. Grants offered subject to conditions which have not been met at the year-end are noted as commitments but not accrued as expenditure.

Source: CC66 SORP 2000 Example Reports and Accounts

Example: Accounting policy

The Diana, Princess of Wales Memorial Fund

Grants payable

Grants payable are accounted for in full as liabilities of the fund when approved by the trustees and accepted by the beneficiaries. The fund monitors the usage to which a grant is put and reports are required from beneficiaries before the next annual instalment is paid. However, the beneficiary would have valid expectation that they would receive the grant as offered and accepted.

Source: Annual Report and Accounts 2001 The Diana, Princess of Wales Memorial Fund

---

Example: Accounting policy

City Parochial Foundation

Grants payable

Grants made for charitable purposes from the Central Fund at the discretion of the trustees, as specified under the terms of the Schemes, are charged to Grants Payable when they are approved by the trustees. When grants are withdrawn or unclaimed they are shown as a deduction from Grants Payable. Grants approved by the trustees not paid at the year-end are carried forward as a liability.

Source: Annual Report and Accounts 2000 The City Parochial Foundation

---

IMPLICATIONS FOR GRANT-MAKING PRACTICE

It is important for the accounting treatment of grants payable to reflect the actual practice of the charity. You may wish to review the way in which grantmaking is undertaken to ensure that this is consistent with the accounting policy you wish to adopt.

For example, if the second and third years of a three-year grant are contingent on successful monitoring, the grant offer letter needs to spell this out clearly. Remember that a moral obligation is established if a valid expectation is created in the mind of the recipient. If you do not wish to accrue the full grant commitment, then you need to make it clear in grant conditions that future instalments are conditional and will not be paid as a matter of course. The accounting treatment follows grantmaking practice.

Some charities rely on future income to make future grant instalments. Therefore, funds may not be available to cover the accrual of commitments for future payments. In this case, it needs to be clear in grant offers that future grant payments are conditional on funding being available. It will then be acceptable to include only the current year's grant payments as expenditure in the accounts.

7 ▼ Managing restricted funds

The structure of funds in charity accounts is an important aspect that makes charities very different to commercial enterprises. Charities have to apply all the funds they receive on their charitable objects, but restricted funds must be applied to the specified purpose.

Restricted funds are funds subject to special trusts specified by the donor. This may be because the donor has attached special conditions to the donation or may be because of the terms of an appeal. For example, a grant may be provided to a charity for use on a specific activity within the overall charitable aims of the charity, or for a particular geographical area. An appeal may be launched by a charity specifically for the purchase of a building and the appeal literature makes it clear that all the funds received through the appeal will be used for that purpose.

A charity's trustees will be in breach of trust if they do not spend restricted funds in accordance with the terms under which the funds were given. This means that the trustees become personally liable to reimburse the charity for the funds spent. Whilst trustees have only had to replace funds on a few occasions, there is a higher risk that a charity will lose credibility with funders should a breach of trust occur. In addition, the Charity Commission have the right to investigate the affairs of a charity in these circumstances, as this may well amount to maladministration.

There are three types of restricted fund:

- Permanent endowment funds
- Expendable endowment funds
- Restricted income funds (frequently termed simply 'restricted funds').

PERMANENT ENDOWMENT FUNDS

Permanent endowment funds are donations that have been given to a charity to be held as capital with no power to convert the funds to income. The charity has to hold the funds in perpetuity, investing them to obtain a return. Usually the income arising will be unrestricted income, unless the terms of the original gift impose restrictions on how the income may be used.

Frequently, permanent endowment funds have been created when a benefactor has left significant funds as a legacy, with instructions that the capital sum should be kept intact.

New permanent endowments should be part of the incoming resources of the charity in the year in which they are receivable. This will be when the funds are actually received, or when the receipt of the funds is certain and the amount known. Endowment funds should have a separate column in the SoFA. Existing permanent endowments where there are no new funds in the year will still need to be shown in the SoFA. The fund balance at the beginning of the year and at the end of the year will need to be shown. The fund is likely to have revaluation gains or losses as a movement on the funds, as investments have to be restated at market value at the balance sheet date.

Illustration: Charity with permanent endowment funds

	Unrestricted funds £	Endowment funds £	This year total £	Last year total £
Incoming resources				
Legacy	-	500,000	500,000	200,000
Investment income	20,000	-	20,000	12,000
Total incoming resources	20,000	500,000	520,000	212,000
Resources expended				
Investment management fees	3,000	3,820	6,820	4,300
Grants payable	15,000		15,000	11,000
Total resources expended	18,000	3,820	21,820	15,300
Net incoming resources	2,000	496,180	498,180	196,700
Unrealised gain on revaluation of investments	-	25,000	25,000	10,000
Net movement in funds	2,000	521,180	523,180	206,700
Funds brought forward at beginning of year	30,000	288,700	318,700	112,000
Funds carried forward at end of year	32,000	809,880	841,880	318,700

The example shows new endowment funds of £500,000 received in the year by way of a legacy. Investment income all goes to the unrestricted funds. One of the functions of good management of investments is to maintain the value of the endowment fund, as demonstrated by the increase in the market value of the funds. The total return on the investments in the year is both the unrealised gain of £25,000 and the investment income of £20,000. In this charity, the whole of the capital gain (unrealised gains) goes to the endowment fund. Therefore the investment manager's fees are apportioned between capital gain and investment income, and allocated to the appropriate funds.

EXPENDABLE ENDOWMENT FUNDS

Expendable endowment funds are donations that have been given to a charity to be held as capital, where the trustees do have a discretionary power to use the funds as income. The terms of the original endowment may set out the circumstances for the funds to be expended, or activities that may be funded.

Generally, expendable endowment funds should be treated in the accounts in the same way as permanent endowment funds. Again, the income arising can be presumed to be unrestricted income. Revaluations will be shown as a movement on funds. However, trustees may use their discretion to allocate capital gains on revaluation between expendable endowment funds and unrestricted income. Trustees wishing to adopt the total return approach to managing their investments will be able to do so without problems where all the endowment funds are expendable. (*See Chapter 5 Investments.*)

If the trustees decide to spend some of the expendable endowment, then the expenditure can be treated in one of two ways:

♦ The expenditure can be shown as part of the resources expended of the endowment fund, with a note to the accounts explaining the circumstances, the nature of the expenditure and any further implications for the funds of the charity. It is likely that the trustees would address this issue in the trustees' annual report as well, especially if the amounts involved are significant.

♦ The amount that the trustees have agreed to release from the endowment fund can be transferred out of the endowment fund into the unrestricted fund. This would be shown in the SoFA on the line for transfers and a note to the accounts would explain the circumstances. The actual expenditure will then be allocated to the unrestricted fund in the resources expended. This method may be more appropriate where the trustees are releasing a fixed amount for spending over a period of time.

Charities may combine the various funds they hold as endowments, showing all fund movements and totals in one column on the SoFA. Further information is needed in a note to the accounts, identifying the major funds and showing the movements in the year. It is good practice to provide a description of each fund and an explanation of how it has arisen. Should a charity have many very small funds of this type, they may group them together in a logical manner. For example, an educational charity may have several donations to a fund to provide a stream of income to pay for bursaries. The description should explain how the charity manages these funds, but it is not necessary to keep every individual fund separate as long as the terms are very similar.

RESTRICTED INCOME FUNDS

Restricted income funds are funds received for a particular purpose to be spent in accordance with the wishes of the donor. Restricted income funds may be raised through an appeal, donations or grants and may be in the form of assets rather than cash.

Restricted income funds are more common, and also provide more challenges to the accountant as the expenditure will need to be tracked through the bookkeeping system in order to both achieve the normal analysis of expenditure and attribute expenditure to particular funds.

It will be necessary to account for each particular fund where this is significant or if the donor has requested it. Donations from different donors may be credited to one restricted fund where the donations are all for the same purpose and on similar terms.

The recording and monitoring of restricted funds can prove a very difficult area for charities of all sizes. Even a relatively small charity can have a number of different restricted funds that may consist of income from more than one donor. In addition, it is becoming increasingly common for donors to request a financial statement of exactly how their money has been spent.

These points emphasise the importance to a charity of being able to demonstrate that funds have been spent in accordance with the donor's wishes. It is therefore essential that a charity has a good system for accounting for its restricted funds.

Recognising restricted funds

In the majority of cases, it is probably clear as to whether the terms attached to a specific donation make that income restricted. If a charity that has a number of different projects receives a grant that the donor states is for a specific project, then this project will have a restricted fund.

However, the same grant given to a charity where the project concerned represents the charity's sole charitable object will not have a restricted fund as there will be no restriction within the overall aims of the charity. It is therefore important to know what the charity's objects in its constitution are. If the objects are narrowly framed, then donations given for purposes set out in the objects are unrestricted. The same donation to another charity with much wider objects would be restricted. It is the responsibility of the trustees of the recipient charity to ensure that they recognise funds in their charity as restricted where appropriate.

Charities sometimes receive grants that are specifically for core funding. Since core funding is meeting the charity's objects, this will usually be seen as unrestricted income. It would only be restricted funding if the application were restricted further, say to certain salaries.

> ### Illustration: Identifying restricted funds
>
> Islington Children's Playgroups is a small charity established to provide educational opportunities for children in the Islington area. They receive a grant from the local authority. In the grant letter, the purpose of the grant is stated as:
>
> 'To provide educational play to children in the Islington area.'
>
> This is funding for the work of the charity and aligned to the charity's objects and so is not restricted.
>
> The charity also receives a grant from BBC Children in Need to fund the salaries of two playworkers in the summer holidays to enable the charity to run a playscheme. This is restricted funding, as the grant must be spent specifically on playworkers' salaries.

Contractual income

One particular grey area concerns contractual arrangements for the delivery of services. It is common for charities to enter into service level agreements with local government bodies, health sector bodies and others. Does this represent a restricted income stream or not?

Such cases need to be considered individually as specific terms may be the determining factor. An indicator may be which party has the right to any unspent funds. If the charity can retain a surplus after proper performance of the service in accordance with the agreement, then this indicates that the income is unrestricted. If the local authority has the right to reclaim unspent funds then this would be an indicator of restricted income.

These are indicators of whether the agreement is truly a contract or really a grant. A contract is a legal undertaking by the charity to provide services in exchange for a contract fee. The charity is selling services as a commercial activity, and so the normal commercial accounting rules apply and this is unrestricted income. Contract fees can still be within the charity's objects, if the activity is fulfilling the primary purpose of the charity. This is known as charitable trading.

The legal restrictions of trust law can only apply to donations and grants. Donations given on the trust that they will be spent on a particular purpose are restricted funds. Contractual payments can be enforced by contract law, not by trust law.

In order to establish whether a particular incoming resource is restricted or not, you need to find out what the terms of the funding are and whether it is to be governed by trust law or contract law. A restricted fund is governed by trust law.

> **Illustration: Contracted income**
>
> Islington Children's Playgroups is asked by the local authority to provide after-school home-work and play facilities. They negotiate a contract for the services, with the local authority agreeing to buy a certain number of hours of childcare for children they refer to the charity.
>
> This is a contract, as the charity is selling a service for a fee. It will therefore be treated as unrestricted income in the charity's accounts and expenditure matched to it.

In summary, restricted income is voluntary income that must be applied for the purposes for which it was given and is governed by trust law. If the fund cannot be applied to the purposes for which it was given, then the trustees must offer to repay the funds to the donor. It is for the donor to decide whether the funds may be applied to another purpose.

Indicators of a restricted fund

- Voluntary funds, that is donations or grants, not a fee for a service
- Funds raised through an appeal, where the appeal literature states a specific purpose of the appeal
- A surplus has to be repaid to the donor (or offered to the donor)
- Terms of donation or grant identify what the funds may be spent on
- Terms define the area for spending the funds more narrowly than the recipient charity's objects.

Deferred income

In certain situations a charity may need to defer some voluntary income as received in advance of the balance sheet date. This will occur if the funding body has imposed specific terms that have to be met before the charity may use the funds. For example, a funding body may specify that a grant can only be spent in a certain timeframe that falls into a future accounting period. This is not the same as the normal delays that can occur between receipt of funds and the related expenditure. In the case where the terms of funding do impose pre-conditions, then the incoming resource should not be recognised in the SoFA until the conditions have been satisfied. If the funds have already been received, then they should be deferred as income received in advance.

Generally, however, funds for a specific purpose should be recognised in full as restricted funds and the unspent balance carried forward. The notes to the accounts need to describe what the funds are for and how the unspent balance will be expended.

This will not apply to earned income of the charity, however, which should be treated in the same way as any commercial operation. A charity receiving contract fees, for example, should treat early payment of fees as income received in advance. This would mean that the receipt is not included in unrestricted income for the accounting period, but instead shown as received in advance in the liabilities on the balance sheet, to be released into income in the appropriate accounting period. Hence it is less likely that the unrestricted funds balance at the balance sheet date will contain funds received in advance. Where this does occur because the charity has raised general donations, the charity may wish to consider whether the funds are to be earmarked for a particular purpose. These funds should then be shown as designated funds.

Funds for the purchase of fixed assets

Some donors provide funds for the purchase of a fixed asset, such as a minibus or a building. This may be as the result of an appeal or it may be a specific grant from one funder. Funds received in this way are for a specified purpose and so are restricted funds. The terms of the funding need to be examined carefully to determine the correct accounting treatment.

Charities commonly raise funds for the purchase of equipment for use in fulfilling their charitable objects. The equipment purchased will be treated as a fixed asset and depreciated over the useful life of the equipment. In commercial accounts, the practice would be to treat the grant income as deferred income that is released over the life of the asset to match depreciation. In charity accounts, the SORP treatment is to show the whole amount of the grant as an incoming resource in the year that it is receivable. It is a restricted fund and the depreciation is charged against that restricted fund. The balance on the fund to be carried forward at the end of each financial year should be the amount needed to fund future depreciation charges. If the grant was only part-funding the assets, the proportions should be maintained throughout the life of the asset.

In certain circumstances, the nature of the restriction will be such that the purpose of the funding has been fulfilled by the purchase of the asset. For example, appeal literature may state that funds are being raised for the purchase of a building. Legally, the restriction is extinguished once the building has been purchased. It is then acceptable to treat the funds received as general funds after the purchase has been made. Since there will be a significant asset on the balance sheet, many charities prefer to treat the funds for this as a designated fund. This shows clearly the relationship between the assets on the balance sheet and the funding for them.

The appropriate treatment will, however, depend on the terms of the funding. A charity may receive grant funding for the purchase of a building for use as a training centre, with conditions attached. These may state that the funder will receive the proceeds from the sale of the building or the equivalent of current market value if the charity ceases to use the building as a training centre. This amounts to an ongoing restriction and it is then correct to retain the funding as restricted funds, with depreciation charged to the fund.

Gifts of fixed assets

A similar situation may arise when charities receive gifts of buildings or other fixed assets for the charity's own use. The terms of the gift are likely to be such that there is an on-going restriction on the use of the asset. It will therefore be appropriate to show the original gift as a new incoming resource into restricted funds, with any depreciation charge shown as an expense in the restricted fund. The balance carried forward at the end of each financial year will represent the net book value of the asset.

Restricted funds in deficit

Situations can arise where a particular restricted fund is in deficit. This can arise because the charity has on-going work in a particular field and it raises funds for this work. It can be difficult to cease the activity temporarily when incoming resources are delayed, particularly if the intention is to continue the activity. When such a situation arises during the year, the trustees have to decide whether they can provide unrestricted funding for the activity in order that the work can continue. It is not acceptable to 'borrow' from other restricted funds, as this is a breach of trust. The likelihood of such a situation arising will influence the trustees' judgement of the need for unrestricted income and reserves.

If the trustees agree to provide temporary funding from unrestricted funds, then there are two possible outcomes. A funder may agree to fund the project in full, and may also reimburse the charity for its temporary funding. This is in effect backdating the funding agreement and this does happen in the case of some government funding. In this situation, it is acceptable to allow the restricted fund to show a deficit, which is later made good by the additional incoming resources coming into the fund. Where such a situation arises at a financial year-end, then the trustees will need to explain the deficit in their report, and explain that incoming resources arising after the balance sheet date will eliminate the deficit.

An alternative outcome is that the new incoming resources may not be backdated and that the unrestricted funding provided as a temporary bridge to allow the project to continue cannot be reimbursed. A permanent transfer from unrestricted funds to restricted funds in the SoFA for the financial year will best show the action taken. If the amount of the transfer is significant the trustees may wish to refer to it in their report. A transfer between funds will need an explanation in the notes to the accounts.

UNRESTRICTED FUNDS IN DEFICIT

The problem of deficits arising in unrestricted funds is more significant. A charity that does not have sufficient incoming resources in its unrestricted funds to cover its unrestricted expenditure is likely to be 'borrowing' from restricted funds. This is a breach of trust, as restricted funds must only be used for the purposes for which they were given.

The charity has to raise more unrestricted incoming resources if it is to continue operations. In the short term, the charity may be able to go to some of the funders providing restricted funds, requesting them to permit the use of the funds on expenditure that does not fall within the original terms of the grant funding. Funders will be sympathetic to this approach if the charity has a good track record in its work and has been entirely open and honest about the position.

In the longer term, the charity needs to redress the balance between restricted and unrestricted funding, to ensure that it does have sufficient unrestricted incoming resources to meet its commitments. In practice, the situation of a deficit on unrestricted funds arises for few reasons:

- Poor financial management, as the situation was one that could have been foreseen.

- Unexpected expenditure arising on unrestricted funds, or a sudden fall in unrestricted income. In practice, this is the purpose of reserves, as they will cushion the charity from the effects of such situations. A charity with a high dependency on restricted funding may well experience a problem if, for example, it has to settle a legal claim. It is unlikely that the terms of restricted funding will allow the charity to use the restricted funding in that case.

- Charities contracted to deliver services may have to pay for redundancy out of their own funds upon termination of the contract if the contract does not provide for this element of cost. In effect, this cost should have been calculated and taken as part of the profit in previous accounting periods.

- The charity may not be allocating costs appropriately to restricted funds. Some charities assume that all management and support costs have to be covered by unrestricted funds. This is not the case, although it is necessary to obtain restricted funds in such a way that they do allow for a contribution towards project management and administration.

Charities experiencing problems may need to review:

- the charity's reserves policy and reserves position;

- the charity's policy on applying for funding for its activities. If it generally receives a large number of restricted funds, it may need to ensure that the funding applications allow for a contribution towards the management and administration costs, so that a part of these can be allocated to restricted funds;

- its level of unrestricted spending and assess the scope for cutting costs;

- how it generates unrestricted income and increase income of this type.

Risk of insolvency

If the deficit on unrestricted funds is large, then this may indicate that the charity is no longer viable. The charity may not use restricted funds for unrestricted expenditure. In order to prevent a breach of trust occurring by spending restricted funds on purposes for which they were not received, the trustees may have to cease operations.

The Charity Commission is likely to investigate any charity submitting annual accounts showing a deficit on unrestricted funds. They may instigate a Section 8 inquiry so that they can protect the balance of restricted funds.

However, it is possible that this position may have come about purely due to timing factors. For example, a one-off liability attributable to unrestricted funds may have to be accrued in the year-end accounts and thus take unrestricted funds into deficit at that point in time. This would not necessarily represent an insolvent position if the charity could demonstrate that the liability would be settled from unrestricted income receivable in the following financial year.

In situations such as this the trustees should clearly explain in their annual report how the position has arisen and how it will be resolved.

MANAGING THE CASHFLOW IMPLICATIONS OF RESTRICTED FUNDS

It has already been noted that charity trustees are in breach of trust if they spend restricted funds on purposes other than those for which the income was originally given. We need to consider how this impacts on the actual cashflow of the charity and how the trustees can minimise the risk of restricted funds being misapplied in this way.

In order to ensure that restricted funds are kept entirely separate from unrestricted funds, some charities hold separate bank accounts for each fund. Occasionally donors have been known to require separate bank accounts. However, this is rare and it is not necessary for charities to do this. In exceptional circumstances where there are serious concerns about the viability of the charity, you might need to track all expenditure to each fund to ensure that a breach of trust does not occur.

Normally, however, the overall cashflow management of a charity does not need to distinguish between restricted and unrestricted cash funds. The important issue is that there are adequate net assets to back each restricted fund.

The cashflow does need careful management for the charity overall, but this applies equally to careful management of restricted funds and unrestricted funds. Key factors to monitor:

◆ The overall cashflow should be regularly forecasted for the next few months. Charities with significant restricted funds should ensure that the overall balance held in cash is sufficient to cover all known commitments and is not likely to lead to borrowing from one fund to pay for expenditure in another fund.

- Restricted funds should be monitored to ensure that they are not overspent.
- The success of incoming resources against target in unrestricted funds should be monitored.

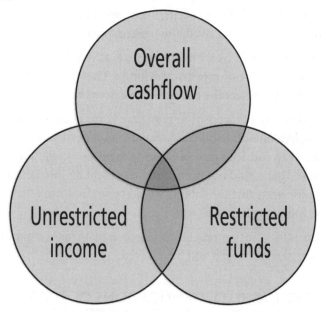

In charities with adequate reserves or a significant proportion of unrestricted income, managing the cashflow implications of restricted funds should not prove a problem. On the other hand, charities with a high dependency on grant funding are likely to have a high proportion of restricted funds and low reserves. The cashflow implications of this financial position need to be considered carefully.

Transfers between funds

Earlier in this chapter, we examined the issue of transferring funds from expendable endowment funds. This is obviously acceptable as long as it is within the terms of the funds.

It is common for funds to be transferred from unrestricted funds to restricted funds. Situations will arise where an activity is mostly a restricted activity, but needs to be subsidised from unrestricted funds. In fact, there are two choices as to how the charity will present this information in the SoFA. It can keep the whole activity with all related expenditure in the restricted column of the SoFA, and then beneath the line 'Net incoming resources' transfer the right amount of unrestricted funds to bring the restricted fund into balance. This will not necessarily be the amount to bring the fund to nil. One particular funder may have provided funds in advance and these may still have to be carried forward into the next financial year.

Less common are transfers from permanent endowment funds and restricted income funds to unrestricted funds. Permanent endowment funds cannot generally be released to unrestricted funds. It is, however, possible that the Charity Commission would consider making a scheme to allow this in exceptional circumstances.

Restricted funds may be transferred to unrestricted funds where they are no longer needed for the restricted purpose and the donor agrees to the transfer. If it is not possible to consult the donor, then it may be necessary to apply to the Charity Commission for a scheme.

EXPLAINING THE MOVEMENT OF FUNDS

The SORP requires the accounts to show the changes in the funds over the year. Whilst this is explained in summary form in the SoFA, further details need to be given in the notes to the accounts. For most charities, this will involve listing the main restricted funds individually and showing the incoming resources and resources expended for each fund, together with any transfers where relevant. Charities with designated funds may wish to give the same information for designated funds. This type of note is a good way of demonstrating clearly what is being done with the funds of the charity.

	Fund balance brought forward	Incoming resources	Resources expended	Transfers	Fund balance carried forward
Restricted funds					
– fund A					
– fund B					
– fund C					
Total restricted funds					

IDENTIFYING ASSETS IN THE FUND

The SORP also requires funds to be explained in terms of the assets and liabilities they represent. This may be important for some charities. For example, if the commitments of a particular fund are fairly immediate, the charity needs to be able to demonstrate that the matching assets are instantly available. Generally, however, it is sufficient to provide information on the overall position, relating to the totals for each type of fund, rather than list every restricted fund individually. A balance sheet drawn up in columnar format would comply with the SORP, but the requirement can equally be satisfied by a note to the accounts.

	Unrestricted funds	Restricted funds	Total
Fixed assets			
Current assets			
Current liabilities			
Long-term liabilities			
Totals			

IDENTIFYING COSTS TO RESTRICTED FUNDS

The costs that should relate to a restricted fund will depend on the purpose of the restricted fund. In certain cases the donor may not specify how the money must be spent beyond saying that it must be spent on a certain project. The SORP states that provided it is not specifically forbidden by the donor then a reasonable allocation of overhead expenses can be set against restricted funds. It should be fair, therefore, to apply the charity's standard cost allocation method to restricted fund activity, as this should represent a reasonable and consistent basis.

For many charities, it is important that they receive a sufficient contribution towards core costs as part of project funding. In order to achieve this in an organisation with high levels of restricted income funds, it should be incorporated in the original funding bids to ensure that the full costs of managing a project can be attributed to the correct fund.

If the charity decides to go ahead with a particular activity, even though the restricted fund is insufficient to cover the indirect costs as well as the direct costs, then the charity may wish to make its subsidy of the activity apparent by transferring unrestricted funds to the relevant restricted fund, with an explanatory note in the notes to the accounts.

Fundraising appeals

It is normal for the costs of the appeal itself to be charged against the income raised in the appeal. Thus, the net resources arising are available for application to the cause set out in the appeal. Care is needed with the wording of the appeal. An appeal that states that 'all donations will be spent on purchasing special equipment for disabled children' will be restricted to applying the money raised to the direct costs of equipment purchase. However, appeals are normally worded more generally to helping with an area of work and it is normal to charge the costs of the appeal against the fund.

Grant funding

It is increasingly common for donors to specify more precisely how their funds should be spent. They may specifically disallow certain types of expenditure and may restrict the allocation of central overheads to a certain percentage. Both management accounts and statutory accounts need to reflect these requirements.

The costs to be set against restricted funds will therefore depend on the terms of the restriction. The process of efficiently managing restricted funds, therefore, needs to start with the budgeting process and the funding applications themselves.

Budgeting

Most charities operate with a mix of restricted and unrestricted income sources. It is highly unlikely that a charity with just restricted income can properly cover all of its indirect or core costs. The annual budget therefore needs to take into account the distinction between restricted and unrestricted income streams. It is no good drawing up a budget with a small and achievable surplus of £20,000 if 90% of the income is restricted and under the terms of the various funding agreements £50,000 of central costs cannot be covered.

Therefore, a charity needs to distinguish between the different funds of the charity when considering how to allocate costs, including central costs, against each restricted fund. This may leave an amount of central costs that will have to be covered by unrestricted income streams. Does the charity expect to receive sufficient unrestricted funding to cover this amount?

It is vital that these issues are thought through and dealt with at the budget setting stage so that potential shortfalls in unrestricted funding can be identified.

Applications for funding

It is clearly beneficial for a charity to be able to maximise the scope for central costs to be covered within its restricted funds. However, for this to be achieved it has to be addressed at the stage of preparing the funding application. Once you are committed to a certain grant agreement it is not possible to change the basis of cost allocations without going back and getting the donor's consent.

It is necessary therefore for the fundraiser or whoever is preparing the funding application to liaise with the finance department before committing the charity to any grant agreement. A funding application for a new project must seek to cover all associated direct costs plus a fair share of central overheads. If a prospective donor refuses to cover these costs then serious consideration should be given as to whether the charity should proceed with the bid.

Recording and monitoring

The accounting systems of a charity need to be designed so that direct expenditure against individual restricted funds can be recorded and reported on when necessary. The level of detail required for reporting depends on the nature of the funding and the funders' requirements.

The most commonly available accounting software systems (for example, Sage, Quickbooks or equivalent) have the capability to record the necessary information. However, some time and thought needs to go into setting the system up appropriately with a good chart of accounts and use of departments and cost centres. Time and a little money spent at the set-up stage to get this structure as tailored as possible to the needs of the charity will be time and money well spent in the long run.

The basic requirements of an accounting system for the purposes of restricted funds are:

◆ to show unspent and overspent balances on a fund by fund basis (distinguishing between restricted and unrestricted funds)

◆ to provide a clear audit trail showing how costs are allocated to individual funds

◆ to produce information to report to donors as and when required.

With a simple system it is probable that to produce some of the necessary information will require some re-analysis by way of spreadsheets. However, with a carefully designed system it should be possible to keep this to a minimum.

CASE STUDY

Borsetshire Mental Health

This case study shows how simple management accounts can be used to monitor restricted funds and how the information may be presented for accounts to comply with SORP.

The restricted funds received by Borsetshire Mental Health in the last year are:

◆ a grant of £50,000 for top-up funding for residential care. This chiefly relates to residents who have been in care for a long period of time and still have preserved rights under old funding systems;

◆ a grant from the local authority for operational costs of the day centres;

◆ a grant of £5,000 from a local grant-making trust for printing some leaflets;

◆ a legacy of £12,000 for residents.

The charity also receives unrestricted funds in the form of contract fees and donations. The total incoming resources for the year are as follows:

	Restricted £	Unrestricted £	Total £
Contract fees for residential care		125,000	125,000
Grant – top-up residential care	50,000		50,000
Grant from LBB for day centres	60,000		60,000
Core funding from LBB		60,000	60,000
Grant from Borsetshire Trust	5,000		5,000
Donations	-	23,726	23,726
Legacies	12,000	-	12,000
Shop sales	-	26,956	26,956
Fundraising	-	23,573	23,573
Bank interest	-	4,700	4,700
Total income	**127,000**	**263,955**	**390,955**

The charity works with the following cost centres, as these are the main areas of activity:

◆ Residential care

◆ Day centres

◆ Information

◆ Shop (selling donated goods to raise funds)

◆ Central support – management and administration for all areas.

The restricted income can therefore be allocated to the cost centres, and these activities can form the basis of a structure for restricted funds:

◆ Top-up grant of £50,000 and legacy should be allocated to residential care.
◆ Local authority grant for day centres should be allocated to day centres.
◆ The trust grant of £5,000 should be allocated to information.

Transferring this information into a format that will start to look like a fund-based income analysis or the top section of the SoFA:

	Restricted	Unrestricted	Total
Donations, legacies and similar	12,000	23,726	35,726
Activities to further the charity's objects			
Residential care	50,000	125,000	175,000
Day centres	60,000		60,000
Information	5,000		5,000
Other		60,000	60,000
Activities to generate funds			
Charity shop		26,956	26,956
Fundraising activities		23,573	23,573
Investment income		4,700	4,700
Total incoming resources	**127,000**	**263,955**	**390,955**

The accounting system they use allows them to code expenditure to the different cost centres using the department code. This means that they do have the direct costs of each activity in the relevant cost centre. They can then undertake an exercise to allocate central support costs to the relevant headings (*see Chapter 8 Allocating costs*). This produces the following information about costs:

	Restricted 2001 £	Unrestricted 2001 £	Total funds 2001 £
Resources expended			
Cost of generating funds			
Charity shop			16,698
Fundraising costs			20,834
Charitable expenditure			
Residential care			200,417
Day centres			56,841
Information			18,623
Support			47,868
Management & admin			9,022
Total resources expended	**-**	**-**	**370,303**

The costs need to be allocated to the funds, as the initial cost allocation exercise considers the allocation into activities. It is reasonable to assume that restricted income is used first for activities, providing the nature of the restriction is well-aligned to the activity being undertaken. For example, this should be reasonable in the case of residential care. The grant of £50,000 is entirely used up during the year to provide services for the residents. The legacy was generally for the residents and so can also be used to fund activities during the year. Care may be needed in similar situations, as the terms of a legacy or donation may define the area of benefit more narrowly. If that were the case, then further work would have to be undertaken to ensure that the money had been used of the purpose for which it was given. If it had not been entirely used, then a balance on restricted funds would have to be carried forward.

The funding for a leaflet has been allocated to the Information activity. The charity needs to ensure that the leaflet was produced in the year and the funds properly applied.

With this information, the allocation of costs to funds can be completed for the current year.

	2001 Restricted £	2001 Unrestricted £	2001 Total funds £
Resources expended			
Cost of generating funds			
Charity shop	-	16,698	16,698
Fundraising costs	-	20,834	20,834
Charitable expenditure			
Residential care	62,000	138,417	200,417
Day centres	56,841		56,841
Information	5,000	13,623	18,623
Support	-	47,868	47,868
Management & admin	-	9,022	9,022
Total resources expended	**123,841**	**246,462**	**370,303**

In this particular example, there is insufficient restricted funding for a contribution to support costs and management and administration costs. However, the terms of the restricted funding should allow the allocation of support costs as a legitimate part of the costs of providing that service. You would need to ensure that the terms did allow the income to be spent on support costs as well as direct costs.

The information can now be pulled together into a SoFA.

Illustration: Borsetshire Mental Health Statement of Financial Activities for the year ending 31 December 2001

	2001 Restricted £	2001 Unrestricted £	2001 Total funds £	2000 Total funds £
Incoming resources				
Donations, legacies and				
similar incoming resources	12,000	23,726	35,726	29,253
Activities to further the charity's objects				
Residential care	50,000	125,000	175,000	
Day centres	60,000	-	60,000	
Information	5,000		5,000	235,000
Other activities	-	60,000	60,000	40,000
Activities to generate funds				
Charity shop	-	26,956	26,956	22,854
Fundraising activities	-	23,573	23,573	12,723
Investment income	-	4,700	4,700	3,955
Total incoming resources	**127,000**	**263,955**	**390,955**	**343,785**
Resources expended				
Cost of generating funds				
Charity shop	-	16,698	16,698	12,792
Fundraising	-	20,834	20,834	8,554
Charitable expenditure				
Residential care	62,000	138,417	200,417	184,565
Day centres	56,841	-	56,841	56,812
Information	5,000	13,623	18,623	18,420
Support	-	47,868	47,868	45,627
Management & admin	-	9,022	9,022	8,272
Total resources expended	**123,841**	**246,462**	**370,303**	**335,042**
Net incoming resources for the year	**3,159**	**17,493**	**20,652**	**8,743**
Funds at 1 January 2001	1,825	20,505	22,330	13,587
Funds at 31 December 2001	**4,984**	**37,998**	**42,982**	**22,330**

As well as producing the SoFA, the preparation of the accounts should produce a note to explain the movement in funds. This work has in effect been covered at the same time as preparing the analysis above.

	Fund balance brought forward	Incoming resources	Resources expended	Transfers	Fund balance carried forward
Restricted funds					
Residential care	-	62,000	62,000	-	-
Day centres	1,825	60,000	56,841	-	4,984
Information	-	5,000	5,000	-	-
Total restricted funds	**1,825**	**127,000**	**123,841**	**-**	**4,984**

Interpreting the accounts

The day centres fund had a small unspent balance of £1,825 brought forward from the previous year plus an on-going restricted grant of £60,000 received in the year. The total of both direct and indirect costs charged to the project in the year was just £56,841, leaving unspent funds at the end of the year of £4,984.

This is potentially causing a problem for the charity as this unspent restricted fund appears to be growing each year.

The information service receives only a small restricted grant of £5,000 for a specific project. Direct costs are £13,857 and allocated indirect costs are £4,766. A large proportion of these costs have to be funded from unrestricted funds, that is through donations or other fundraising. Another way of showing this would have been to show the full costs of the information service in restricted funds, with just the grant contributing directly to these costs. The deficit on this fund could then be offset by a transfer from unrestricted funds. If this option were chosen, it would clearly demonstrate that the excess of project-related costs over the project-related income is in effect being covered from unrestricted funds.

8 ▼ Allocating costs

The SORP requires charities to provide information about the costs of their activities. Rather than a list of account headings, charities are required to allocate costs to activities. The categories of expenditure are:

- ◆ cost of generating funds
- ◆ charitable expenditure:
  - – grants payable in furtherance of the charity's objects
  - – costs of activities in furtherance of the charity's objects
  - – support costs
  - – management and administration of the charity.

Charities can amend the headings to some extent to fit their activities. The two main headings are compulsory. So a charity could develop headings for its SoFA as follows:

Resources expended

    Cost of generating funds
        Charity shop
        Fundraising and publicity

    Charitable expenditure
        Activities to further the charity's objects
            Advice and information
            Outreach work
            Training project
            Support costs
        Management & administration of the charity

This is just an example; each charity will need to consider appropriate headings that reflect the work of the charity. The expenditure headings should also link to the income headings, so that a reader can see how an activity is funded. The trustees' annual report should also be consistent with the income and expenditure headings in its description of the charity's activities.

COST OF GENERATING FUNDS

The cost of generating funds are the costs of obtaining funds for the charity's work, such as advertising, direct mail, staff time and agents' fees. It can include the raising of donations, and also the sales of goods or services if the purpose is to raise funds, such as selling Christmas cards. It will also include negotiating contracts or bids for new work, although the cost of monitoring and reporting progress on such contracts would usually be seen as part of the support costs of the work funded by the contract.

The headings used under the compulsory heading of 'Cost of generating funds' are at the charity's discretion. The most significant activities to generate funds should be included as separate lines. You may group together several activities under one heading, such as 'fundraising events', if appropriate.

You should use headings that can be matched to the income categories under 'Activities to generate funds' in the SoFA as far as possible. It is recognised that there will probably need to be a general category for fundraising costs to reflect the staff time on planning and managing activities and overall fundraising effort.

Publicity to raise the charity's profile should be included in this category, but not advertising to promote the charity's objects or to educate people about the cause. For example, advertising to recruit volunteers or new pupils to a school should be seen as part of the charitable activities of the charity. Advertising a jumble sale to raise funds would be part of the cost of generating funds. Publicity to promote the charity's objects is likely to be targeted at beneficiaries or others who can use the information to further the charity's objectives.

Information targeted at potential donors (rather than potential beneficiaries) should be part of the cost of generating funds, even where it provides general information about the charity's activities.

Fundraising costs should not be netted off against income. Where a subsidiary company is used to undertake some of the charity's fundraising activities, the costs of those activities would have to be included under the cost of generating funds in the consolidated SoFA.

Investment management fees are included under the cost of generating funds.

It is likely that the cost of generating funds will consist of direct costs, such as the costs of fundraising events, and an element of apportioned staff and overhead costs of the whole organisation. We examine the basis for such apportionments in detail further on in this chapter.

The SORP provides the option of showing a sub-total for total income less the cost of generating funds, termed 'net incoming resources available for charitable application'.

Illustration: Statement of Financial Activities for the year ended 31 March 2002

	Restricted £	Unrestricted £	2002 Total £	2001 Total £
Incoming resources				
Activities to further charity's objects	150,000	95,535	**245,535**	207,304
Activities to generate funds				
Charity shop	-	19,465	**19,465**	17,242
Donations	5,000	-	**5,000**	6,796
Investment income	765	900	**1,665**	1,324
Total incoming resources	**155,765**	**115,900**	**271,665**	**232,666**
Resources expended				
Cost of generating funds				
Charity shop	-	14,773	**14,773**	11,225
Fundraising and publicity	-	4,079	**4,079**	1,893
Total cost of generating funds	-	**18,852**	**18,852**	**13,118**
Net incoming resources available for charitable application	155,765	97,048	**252,813**	219,548
Charitable expenditure				
Activities to further charity's objects				
Advice and information	67,008	-	**67,008**	59,876
Outreach work	68,391	-	**68,391**	53,316
Training project	-	80,836	**80,836**	63,606
Management & administration of the charity	1,250	8,827	**10,077**	7,372
Total charitable expenditure	**136,649**	**89,663**	**226,312**	**184,170**
Total resources expended	**136,649**	**108,515**	**245,164**	**197,288**
Net incoming resources for the year	**19,116**	**7,385**	**26,501**	**35,378**

CHARITABLE EXPENDITURE

Grants payable in furtherance of the charity's objects

Some charities achieve their objectives by making grants to other organisations or to individuals. Where grantmaking is a significant activity to the charity, then the SoFA should show grants payable as a line and show the amounts distributed. The administrative costs of grantmaking will be shown under support costs or management and administration.

Further detailed information on the accounting treatment for grantmaking activities is given in Chapter 6 Grantmaking.

Costs of activities in furtherance of the charity's objects

These are the main costs under charitable expenditure for many charities providing services. Charities may choose whether they use the exact words as a sub-heading or whether they omit that sub-heading. What they must do is give some analysis of the expenditure to fit the activities of the charity. For clarity, there should be a clear link between the stated charitable aims of the charity, as set out in its governing documents, and the actual activity areas. At the end of this chapter we have set out in full a worked example of cost allocation. In that example, three specific activity areas have been identified and these are shown separately on the face of the SoFA:

+ Provision of residential care for those suffering from mental illness

+ Costs of a day centre offering support to the target group

+ Information service providing help to families of individuals with mental illness and educating the general public.

There should be consistency between these activity areas and the activities in furtherance of the charity's objects under incoming resources. However, there may not be an exact match as, for example, there may be some activity areas that do not directly generate any income, but are supported through donations and grants.

The notes to the accounts should give an analysis of the main components of the activity costs. This is likely to be a note that gives the breakdown of the activity costs into headings such as staff costs, office costs, communication costs and so on.

Support costs

The SORP defines support costs as costs incurred directly in support of expenditure on the objects of the charity. Frequently, support costs are the costs of managing and administering projects. It may be appropriate to identify the support costs in one heading because the structure of the charity means that these functions are provided from a central office. Alternatively, a charity may have a system of allocating such costs to the individual projects or areas of activity.

Support costs can include the costs of the various 'support services' of a charity, such as head office costs and the salary of finance and administration staff. These costs can be seen as integral to the direct charitable objects as without these services the charitable activities could not be performed.

The support costs should be shown on the face of the SoFA where these are material. They can be absorbed into the costs of activities where they are not material. In either case, an analysis of the support costs should be given in the notes to the accounts. This should show the breakdown into salaries, rent, rates and so on.

103

Management and administration costs of the charity

Management and administration costs of the charity are distinct from the management and administration of the projects and charitable activities. This category includes the costs of statutory compliance, governance and strategic level management. Examples of direct costs that would be covered under this heading include external audit fees, the cost of internal audit, the costs of trustee meetings and the production of the annual accounts. A charity may also have legal costs, costs of other advice and possible restructuring or re-organisation costs.

Governance and statutory compliance will involve some element of staff time for most charities, and a fair proportion of office costs should also be allocated to this category.

The notes to the accounts should give an analysis of the main components of the management and administration costs. This note will give a breakdown into headings such as staff costs, office costs, communication costs and so on.

PREPARING CHARITY ACCOUNTS

Many charities will only wish to prepare a SoFA once a year for the published financial accounts. Some charities may produce something similar for the management accounts, but most charities will present the management accounts in a slightly different format. The starting point for preparing the SoFA will usually be the management accounts. The requirements of the SORP do have implications for the way in which management accounts are prepared and basic bookkeeping records maintained. One of the main requirements of the SORP is to present activity-based expenditure on the face of the SoFA, but further analysis in the natural cost headings in the notes to the accounts. This means that you still have to be able to provide an analysis of costs into headings such as salaries, telephone, premises costs and so on. Your system needs to be able to cope with two-way analysis.

Direct and indirect costs

Within each of the required SoFA headings there will be a mix of both direct and indirect costs. Direct costs are usually easy to identify. For example, the salary cost of a fundraiser would be a direct cost under the cost of generating funds heading; repairs and maintenance on a care home would be a direct cost under residential care.

Indirect costs are harder to deal with and it is these that require a method of cost allocation. They may include the salary cost of a project worker who works on two different activity areas or the rent on the head office. What is the most appropriate basis to apportion these costs?

The distinction between direct and indirect costs has implications for how the day-to-day bookkeeping of a charity is performed, and also for the presentation of expenditure in management and statutory accounts. Most accounting software systems will allow for appropriate coding structures and cost centre analysis to record direct costs. Indirect costs are most usefully gathered into one cost centre of their own, such as 'central costs'. These will be all the costs that relate to more than one activity. They can then be apportioned to activities on a periodic basis when management accounts are required.

Apportioning indirect costs

Before a charity can prepare its statutory accounts it needs to develop a basis for apportioning indirect costs over the agreed SoFA headings for expenditure.

The SORP recognises that there will be a need for cost apportionment and states that this should be carried out on a 'reasonable, justifiable and consistent basis'.

The basis used should aim to reflect the use made by each activity area of management time, administrative support, premises and central services.

To provide the most accurate picture possible, each account heading could be considered separately and the most appropriate basis applied to each heading. For example, rent on the premises occupied by the charity could be apportioned on the basis of the amount of floor space used by each activity. Stationery costs may best be allocated on the basis of the number of staff and volunteers working on an activity.

However, it should be recognised that the basis of apportionment in any situation will be an estimate and the SORP only requires a 'reasonable' basis to be applied. In many cases, therefore, it will be acceptable to apply a single method of apportionment to all indirect costs.

Some of the more common methods of apportionment include:

- staff numbers
- staff time
- staff costs
- number of clients or beneficiaries
- space occupied.

A method based on staff numbers is particularly appropriate for more staff intensive activities.

Staff time is a good basis for allocating central salaries such as the chief executive or finance manager, particularly if a timesheet exercise is undertaken.

Staff costs may produce a similar result to staff time, but avoids the need to have detailed time records. You would need to be able to identify the majority of staff to particular activities as direct costs to be able to use this method.

Number of clients or beneficiaries is a useful method if the number of clients assisted reflects the number of staff and other resources required.

Space occupied is a good basis if the cost of premises is a major cost element to be apportioned. It will also be helpful if there is a marked difference between the types of activities. For example, a training workshop for building trades may occupy a considerable amount of space and use a great deal of power. The fundraising department, by contrast, may use little space or power, but have high levels of staff costs. You may need to look at the basis of apportionment for two or three major areas of costs in such a situation and apply two different methods.

The most appropriate basis will depend on the individual charity and the type of costs being apportioned. It is important to identify the main cost 'drivers' for an activity. For many charities, a large proportion of total expenditure is staff related. It therefore makes sense to use a method of apportioning costs that is based on staff time or costs.

In order to prepare charity accounts, you need to undertake the cost allocation exercise at an early stage. This should lead to preparation of the notes to the accounts first, and then preparation of the SoFA. It saves a lot of time and effort if the accounts preparation is undertaken in this order, as changes to the allocations will change all the other presentation.

The expenditure analysis is a matrix exercise, as costs have to be allocated across activities as well as identified to the different funds of the charity. The note to the accounts that explains the movement on funds should be completed alongside the cost allocations before the SoFA and balance sheet are finalised.

Notes to the accounts

The accounting policies should explain the basis for including items in:

- the cost of generating funds
- the costs of activities in furtherance of the charity's objects
- support costs
- management and administration of the charity.

Example: Accounting policy

Fundraising expenses include the salaries and overhead costs of the staff who undertake fundraising activities.

Management and administration expenses represent the salaries, direct expenditure and overhead costs of central servicing departments at head office, such as Corporate Finance and Corporate Human Resources, net of any appropriate recharge to the operational divisions.

Source: Oxfam annual report and accounts 2001/2002

An accounting policy note is also required to explain the methods and principles for the allocation and apportionment of costs. This should explain the method used, such as staff time, staff salaries and so on, as appropriate. The policy should provide information on the proportions used in the allocation where the costs apportioned are significant.

Example: Accounting policy

Resources expended are allocated to each activity where the cost relates directly to that activity. The cost of overall direction and administration of each activity, comprising the salary and overhead costs of the central function, is apportioned on the following basis which is an estimate, based on staff time, of the amount attributable to each activity.

	%
Charity shop	0
Fundraising and publicity	15
Advice and information	20
Outreach work	20
Training project	30
Management and administration of the charity	15

Source: CC66 SORP 2000; Example Reports and Accounts

Other notes to the accounts need to give information about the breakdown of the costs. The SoFA itself is really a summary, drawing together various information. Further detail is required in the notes to the accounts. The SORP specifically requires further analysis of:

- the major items of expenditure for each area of charitable activity
- support costs
- costs of managing and administering the charity.

This can be presented in a number of ways. The example accounts from the Charity Commission provide several examples of how this might be done:

Example: Analysis of costs
The Rosanna Grant Trust

Support costs	2001 £'000	2000 £'000
Staff costs	63	54
Office rental and costs	25	19
Computer costs	17	4
Depreciation	5	4
	110	81

Management and administration		
Staff costs	11	10
Office rental and costs	25	19
Auditor's fees for audit services	5	4
Auditor's fees for other services	1	-
Legal fees	10	12
Computer costs	6	6
Costs of meetings	6	10
Depreciation	2	2
	66	63

Source: CC66 SORP 2000: Example Reports and Accounts

Example: Analysis of Costs
The ABC Charity – Total resources expended

	Staff costs £'000	Other direct costs £'000	Other allocated costs £'000	2001 Total £'000	2000 Total £'000
Fundraising costs	210	360	120	690	550
Building appeal costs	25	5	15	45	110
Merchandising costs	80	560	230	870	1,040
Investment management fees	-	90	-	90	110
Residential care costs	2,000	330	100	2,430	2,545
Childcare	2,800	345	255	3,400	3,150
Emergency services	1,980	870	250	3,100	2,800
Information and education	25	65	10	100	300
Support costs	45	110	35	190	50
Management and administration	85	145	40	270	230
Total resources expended	**7,250**	**2,880**	**1,055**	**11,185**	**10,885**

Source: CC66 SORP 2000: Example Reports and Accounts

Tips on cost allocation

Keep it simple

Decide on some activity headings that will last for many years. There is no need to go into excessive detail on the face of the SoFA, and there is no need to list every project. Group projects into areas of activity that you can report on consistently from one year to the next.

Select a simple allocation method

It is easy to get bogged down in too much detail when devising a method for cost allocation. Remember that the basis used only needs to be 'reasonable, consistent and justifiable'. It does not need to be 100% accurate. Identify one basis that is most appropriate and stick to it.

Identify direct costs as far as possible

This reduces the extent to which apportionment is required and therefore will result in a more accurate result. This will also assist in the recording of restricted funds. Any of the basic accounting software systems can report on a cost centre basis that allows direct costs to be allocated to a particular project area at the time they are entered onto the system.

Avoid too many cost centres

Consistency between the headings for the management accounts and the statutory accounts allows the transfer of financial information from one form of accounts to the other with the minimum of re-analysis. Too many cost centres increases the scope for errors at the point of entry into the system and can create extra work in the production of statutory accounts.

Transparency

A single matrix note in the accounts clearly shows how all the natural cost headings relate to the SoFA. A clear transparent accounting policy also assists the reader understand the charity better and gives people more confidence in your charity.

Consistency

Whatever method you choose, stick with it. Consistency from one year to the next will at least ensure that the accounts are comparable. Try to agree a method that basically works and then stick with it. It is even better if this is consistent with the method used in your budgets.

CASE STUDY

Borsetshire Mental Health is a small local charity with the following charitable activities:

◆ Provision of residential care for those suffering from mental illness
◆ Costs of a day centre offering support to the target group
◆ Information service providing help to families of individuals with mental illness and educating the general public.

It also has a small shop and a part-time fundraiser.

It uses a basic cost centre accounting system with five separate cost centres:

◆ Residential care
◆ Day centres
◆ Information
◆ Shop
◆ Central support.

Its management accounts for the year ending 31 December 2001 are shown below. The costs shown in these accounts are all direct costs before any apportionment of central costs or overheads are made. For example, the residential care salary costs of £68,723 reflect the cost of employees working exclusively within the care home. The amounts for rent reflect the rent paid for the care home (£25,000), the shop (£5,000), and head office (£20,000), respectively.

All costs not directly relating to the three charitable activity areas or the shop are shown as central support costs. These include the salary costs of the chief executive and finance and administration staff.

The income streams associated with each activity area are also shown. Where income is received for a specific activity, this is allocated to that cost centre. This type of income is also most likely to be restricted income. Other income sources, such as unrestricted grants and fundraising proceeds, are shown under central support.

Illustration: Borsetshire Mental Health Management accounts for year ending 31 December 2001

	Residential care £	Day centres £	Information £	Shop £	Central support £	Total £
Income						
Grants	125,000	60,000	5,000	-	60,000	250,000
Contract income	50,000	-	-	-	-	50,000
Donations	-	-	-	-	23,726	23,726
Legacies	12,000	-	-	-	-	12,000
Shop sales	-	-	-	26,956	-	26,956
Fundraising	-	-	-	-	23,573	23,573
Bank interest	-	-	-	-	4,700	4,700
Total income	**187,000**	**60,000**	**5,000**	**26,956**	**111,999**	**390,955**
Expenditure						
Salaries	68,723	33,467	12,465	-	84,046	198,701
Agency staff	42,565	-	-	-	-	42,565
Training	4,332	1,673	-	-	-	6,005
Travel	1,663	402	-	-	198	2,263
Recruitment	3,352	886	-	-	-	4,238
Volunteers' expenses	803	1,486	-	4,422	-	6,711
Social events	1,472	-	-	-	-	1,472
Catering	10,837	3,124	-	-	-	13,961
Cleaning	568	145	-	243	-	956
Rent	25,000	-	-	5,000	20,000	50,000
Heat & light	3,589	-	-	1,296	2,456	7,341
Water rates	2,472	-	-	403	1,240	4,115
Depreciation	5,264	1,347	667	-	-	7,278
Equipment	1,282	496	-	307	-	2,085
Insurance	1,236	434	-	635	-	2,305
Advertising	-	-	-	-	3,348	3,348
Printing	-	-	725	-	-	725
Telephone	3,756	-	-	588	2,113	6,457
Postage	-	-	-	-	2,132	2,132
Stationery	-	-	-	-	2,863	2,863
Trustee expenses	-	-	-	-	282	282
Accountancy & audit	-	-	-	-	4,500	4,500
Total expenditure	**176,914**	**43,460**	**13,857**	**12,894**	**123,178**	**370,303**
Surplus/Deficit	**10,086**	**16,540**	**(8,857)**	**14,062**	**(11,179)**	**20,652**

Central staff costs of £84,046 consist of the following salaries (including employer's national insurance and employer's pension contributions where applicable):

111

	£
Director	32,550
Finance and admin manager	23,825
Administrator	14,673
Fundraiser (part-time)	12,998
Total	**84,046**

An exercise was then undertaken to estimate approximately how much time each of these staff members spent during the year working directly on seven different activities represented by the SoFA headings. This produced the following outcome:

	Director	Finance and admin manager	Administrator	Fundraiser
Residential care	30%	-	-	-
Day centres	20%	-	-	-
Information	5%	-	5%	-
Shop	-	10%	5%	-
Support	35%	75%	80%	-
Management and administration	5%	5%	5%	-
Cost of generating funds	5%	10%	5%	100%
Total	**100%**	**100%**	**100%**	**100%**

This information was then applied to the salary costs of each staff member and a total of central staff cost for each activity heading was achieved.

	Director	Finance and	Administrator admin manager	Fundraiser
Residential care	9,765	-	-	-
Day centres	6,510	-	-	-
Information	1,628	-	734	-
Shop	-	2,383	734	-
Support	11,391	17,869	11,737	-
Management and administration	1,628	1,191	734	-
Cost of generating funds	1,628	2,382	734	12,998
Total	**32,550**	**23,825**	**14,673**	**12,998**

The management accounts also show that residential care, day centres and information all had direct staff costs. Adding the direct staff costs to the allocated indirect staff costs gives total staff costs as follows:

	Residential care	Day centres	Information	Shop	Support	Mgt & admin	Cost of generating funds	Total
Director	9,765	6,510	1,628	-	11,391	1,628	1,628	32,550
Finance & admin manager	-	-	-	2,383	17,869	1,191	2,382	23,825
Administrator	-	-	734	734	11,737	734	734	14,673
Fundraiser (P/T)	-	-	-	-	-	-	12,998	12,998
Total central salaries	9,765	6,510	2,362	3,117	40,997	3,553	17,742	84,046
Add: direct salary costs	68,723	33,467	12,465	-	-	-	-	114,655
Total salary costs	78,488	39,977	14,827	3,117	40,997	3,553	17,742	198,701
Percentage of total salary costs per cost centre:	40%	20%	7%	2%	20%	2%	9%	100%

These final percentages can then be applied to all the other central costs to allocate these across the seven SoFA headings. For example, 40% of the postage cost is allocated to residential care, 20% to day centres and so on. There are some exceptions to this as certain costs fall wholly within one category. For example, trustee expenses are allocated entirely to management and administration, as this relates to the reimbursement of their travel costs for attending trustee meetings. This produces an allocation of central costs as in the following chart.

Illustration: Borsetshire Mental Health Allocation of central costs for year ending 31 December 2001

	Total central costs £	Residential care (40%) £	Day centres (20%) £	Information (7%) £	Shop (2%) £	Support (20%) £	Management & admin (2%) £	Fundraising (9%) £
Salaries (per salary allocation)	84,046	9,765	6,510	2,362	3,117	40,997	3,553	17,742
Travel	198	78	40	14	4	40	4	18
Rent	20,000	8,000	4,000	1,400	400	4,000	400	1,800
Heat & light	2,456	982	491	172	49	491	49	222
Water rates	1,240	496	248	87	25	248	25	111
Advertising	3,348	1,339	670	234	67	670	67	301
Telephone	2,113	845	423	148	42	423	42	190
Postage	2,132	853	426	149	43	426	43	192
Stationery	2,863	1,145	573	200	57	573	57	258
Trustee expenses	282	-	-	-	-	-	282	-
Accountancy & audit	4,500	-	-	-	-	-	4,500	-
Total	**123,178**	**23,503**	**13,381**	**4,766**	**3,804**	**47,868**	**9,022**	**20,834**

We can then add this to the information on direct costs for the various activities to produce a detailed note on the resources expended.

Illustration: Borsetshire Mental Health Total resources expended for year ending 31 December 2001

	Residential care £	Day centres £	Information £	Shop £	Support £	Management & admin £	Fundraising £	Total £
Salaries (per salary allocation)	78,488	39,977	14,827	3,117	40,997	3,553	17,742	198,701
Agency staff	42,565	-	-	-	-	-	-	42,565
Training	4,332	1,673	-	-	-	-	-	6,005
Travel	1,741	442	14	4	40	4	18	2,263
Recruitment	3,352	886	-	4,422	-	-	-	4,238
Volunteers' expenses	803	1,486	-	-	-	-	-	6,711
Social events	1,472	-	-	-	-	-	-	1,472
Catering	10,837	3,124	-	243	-	-	-	13,961
Cleaning	568	145	-	-	-	-	-	956
Rent	33,000	4,000	1,400	5,400	4,000	400	1,800	50,000
Heat & light	4,571	491	172	1,345	491	49	222	7,341
Water rates	2,968	248	87	428	248	25	111	4,115
Depreciation	5,264	1,347	667	-	-	-	-	7,278
Equipment	1,282	496	-	307	-	-	-	2,085
Insurance	1,236	434	-	635	-	-	-	2,305
Advertising	1,339	670	234	67	670	67	301	3,348
Printing	-	-	725	630	-	-	-	725
Telephone	4,601	423	148	630	423	42	190	6,457
Postage	853	426	149	43	426	43	192	2,132
Stationery	1,145	573	200	57	573	57	258	2,863
Trustee expenses	-	-	-	-	-	282	-	282
Accountancy & audit	-	-	-	-	-	4,500	-	4,500
Total	200,417	56,841	18,623	16,698	47,868	9,022	20,834	370,303
These are made up of:								
Direct costs	176,914	43,460	13,857	12,894	-	-	-	247,125
Central allocated costs	23,503	13,381	4,766	3,804	47,868	9,022	20,834	123,178
Total	200,417	56,841	18,623	16,698	47,868	9,022	20,834	370,303

This can be summarised further to produce a note to go in the published accounts, summarising all the account headings for premises into one line, for example.

This information will then feed into the SoFA, allowing completion of the expenditure information in the total column for the year. At this stage, the work has not been taken a stage further to analyse this information into the different funds of the charity. This is examined in Chapter 7 Managing restricted funds.

Illustration: Borsetshire Mental Health

Extract from Statement of Financial Activities for the year ending 31 December 2001

	Restricted 2001 £	Unrestricted 2001 £	Total funds 2001 £	Total funds 2000 £
Resources expended				
Cost of generating funds				
Charity shop			16,698	12,792
Fundraising costs			20,834	8,554
Charitable expenditure				
Residential care			200,417	184,565
Day centres			56,841	56,812
Information			18,623	18,420
Support			47,868	45,627
Management & admin			9,022	8,272
Total resources expended	-	-	**370,303**	**335,042**

The notes to the accounts will require an accounting policy to explain the basis under which costs are allocated in the accounts.

Illustration: Accounting policy for allocation of costs

Resources expended are allocated to each activity where the cost relates directly to that activity. The cost of overall direction and administration of each activity, comprising the salary and overhead costs of the central function, is apportioned on the following basis, which is an estimate, based on staff time, of the amount attributable to each activity.

	%
Charity shop	2
Fundraising	9
Residential care	40
Day centres	20
Information	7
Supports costs	20
Management and administration	2

---

9 ▼ Tangible fixed assets

Financial Reporting Standard (FRS) 15 was issued in 1999, and covers the cost, valuation and depreciation of tangible fixed assets. This applies to charities just as much as it applies to commercial companies, as do all standards. FRS 15 does not cover investment assets, but is concerned with the assets an organisation uses in its operations. SORP 2000 has been updated for FRS 15, and now provides additional explanations of ways in which the FRS can be applied to charities. In addition, charities may have to consider the effect of FRS 11 relating to the impairment of fixed assets. This is explained further on in this chapter.

Tangible fixed assets are the buildings and equipment a charity owns. They are usually larger items and held for the long-term, rather than stock, which is held for resale. Intangible assets, by contrast, do not have physical substance and are assets such as patents, rights and intellectual property. The rights to receive royalties on a book or film are intangible assets, for example. In this chapter we are concerned with buildings and equipment.

CAPITALISATION LIMIT

To be treated as tangible fixed assets, the items need to be substantial in value. For example, a plastic in-tray for a desk is a physical asset that will be used for a number of years. However, if all such assets costing just a few pounds are treated as fixed assets, the resulting accounting entries will be too complex.

Instead, you should set a limit to the cost of items you will treat as fixed assets; items below this limit will be treated as operating expenditure through the SoFA.

The level set will mainly depend upon the size of your organisation. A charity with total incoming resources of approximately £100,000, for example, may want to capitalise (treat as fixed assets) all items costing more than £100. This would not be appropriate for a charity with a turnover in excess of £5 million, where a limit of £5,000, for example, may be more appropriate.

There is no set rule on the capitalisation limit that you should choose. This is a decision that should be agreed by the trustees and disclosed in the accounting policy on fixed assets. Remember that you need to keep a detailed inventory of all assets, including those not capitalised, to facilitate their safekeeping and insurance.

TREATMENT OF FIXED ASSETS

The balance sheet should show fixed assets subdivided between:

- intangible assets
- tangible assets
- inalienable and historic assets
- investments.

FRS 15 and the SORP require that all tangible fixed assets be capitalised on initial acquisition and included in the balance sheet at cost or valuation. Most tangible fixed assets are the assets held for the charity's own use. Frequently, charities also hold historic and inalienable assets. These two categories of assets will be dealt with separately.

MIXED USE OF FIXED ASSETS

Some charities have land and buildings that they use partly for their own use (as a functional asset) and partly lease out as an investment. The treatment of these buildings in the accounts should reflect the primary purpose for holding them. So, if only a small part of the asset is leased out or the lease is only for a short time, then the whole asset can be treated as a tangible fixed asset. Similarly, if the majority of the building is an investment, it should be treated as such in the accounts. If the use is more evenly split, then the balance sheet will need to include a split between functional and investment assets.

COST OF TANGIBLE FIXED ASSETS

The cost of a tangible fixed asset is defined as the initial purchase price (after any trade discounts), plus any costs directly attributable to bringing the assets into working condition, such as stamp duty, delivery costs and professional fees. For example, a charity buying a building may incur legal fees for the conveyancing and surveyor's fees to obtain a survey on the building prior to purchase. These are all part of the costs of acquiring the building.

Subsequent expenditure on fixed assets should be capitalised where the performance of the asset is enhanced, rather than just maintained. For example, building works may be capitalised when they are improvements rather than simply repairs.

DEPRECIATION OF TANGIBLE FIXED ASSETS

Depreciation is a measure of the consumption or wearing-out of an asset through the passage of time, use or obsolescence. The original cost or valuation of the asset is spread over its useful economic life. Depreciation is charged annually to the SoFA. This is a way of charging an appropriate amount each year as an operating cost to represent the cost of wear and tear of that asset. This is fairer than charging the whole amount of a major purchase to operating costs in year one, when in fact it is going to be used by the organisation for a number of years.

Illustration: Depreciation

A wildlife charity running a visitors' centre is expanding and is opening a shop to sell bought-in goods to visitors. You spend £10,000 fitting the shop out, in anticipation that this will help to produce future income. We have to estimate how long we think the equipment and so on will last and generate income. If we estimate five years, then depreciation can be estimated as £10,000, divided by 5, equalling £2,000 per year.

In other words, the estimated cost of the wear and tear on shop fittings is £2,000 each year for 5 years. This is fairer than trying to recover the total cost of fitting out in the first year.

The cost of an asset is shown in the balance sheet, less the accumulated depreciation to that date. This is the net book value of the asset at the date of that balance sheet. At the end of an asset's expected useful life, it has nil net book value. This does not necessarily mean that it will not be usable, but simply that further use is a 'bonus'. If the estimated useful life changes during an asset's life, you should consider changing the depreciation. However, this would not be necessary unless the effect on the accounts was significant.

The most common method of depreciation is the straight line method. This is the method used in the example above, where the original cost is spread evenly over the life of the asset and the cost is simply divided by the number of years of the estimated useful life.

The reducing balance method is an alternative method. It uses a percentage of the net book value to calculate the depreciation each year. Taking the above example of shop fittings, we are still working on the assumption that the shop fittings will last approximately 5 years. On the reducing balance method, the nearest approximation is then 25% per year. The calculations over the life will be:

Original cost	10,000
Depreciation in year 1 – 25% of £10,000	2,500
Net book value at the end of year 1	7,500
Depreciation in year 2 – 25% of £7,500	1,875
Net book value at the end of year 2	5,625
Depreciation in year 3 – 25% of £5,625	1,406
Net book value at the end of year 3	4,219
Depreciation in year 4 – 25% of £4,219	1,055
Net book value at the end of year 4	3,164
Depreciation in year 5 – 25% of £3,164	791
Net book value at the end of year 5	2,373

Using the reducing balance method, the net book value never goes down to nil. The amount of depreciation charged to the SoFA is less each year. Some people prefer this method; they believe it matches reality better, as assets often lose more value in the early years and then require more maintenance in later years. This may well be true for vehicles, but is not necessarily true for all assets.

You need to state in your accounting policy for depreciation which method you are using.

It is also common to depreciate assets for a full year in the financial year in which they are acquired. So even if an asset is purchased halfway through a financial year, you would still calculate the depreciation as if you had had the asset for a full year. However, this is a matter of choice. It is possible to make proportional calculations so that the depreciation amount reflects the number of months the asset was owned in the financial year. The only important point is to be consistent with all calculations in one organisation, and to keep adequate records so that you can see when the accumulated depreciation is equal to the original cost of the asset.

Illustration: Depreciation

Your organisation buys a minibus, which is used for transporting residents to day centres and on visits. The minibus cost £24,000 and you estimate that it has a useful life of four years. This will appear in the balance sheet as follows:

Balance Sheet

	£
End of Year 1 (Extract)	
Fixed asset – cost	24,000
Depreciation to date	(6,000)
Net book value	18,000
End of Year 2 (Extract)	
Fixed asset – cost	24,000
Depreciation to date	(12,000)
Net book value	12,000
End of Year 3 (Extract)	
Fixed asset – cost	24,000
Depreciation to date	(18,000)
Net book value	6,000
End of Year 4 (Extract)	
Fixed asset – cost	24,000
Depreciation to date	24,000
Net book value	-

Useful life

In order to agree an accounting policy for depreciation, you need to assess the useful life of the assets involved. This is the length of time that your charity will derive some economic benefit from the asset.

Different groups of assets will have a different expected useful life. Computers, for example, may not last as long as office furniture. Remember that the useful life is only an estimate, so it does not matter if it is not precise. There are some general points that can help in assessing the useful life:

- Leasehold improvements are usually depreciated over the life of the lease.
- Freehold buildings and improvements tend to be depreciated over a longer period, perhaps 50 years.
- Vehicles are generally assumed to last four years.
- Computer equipment is often assumed to last three years.

The main factor, however, is that the useful life should be based on reasonable assumptions relating to your charity's circumstances. For example, if you know that minibuses are always kept in service for at least eight years, then the economic life should reflect this and not be set at four years because that is the norm.

Where a fixed asset for charity use comprises two or more major components with substantially different useful lives, each component should be accounted for as a separate asset and depreciated over its useful economic life. For example, the lift in a building may be depreciated over a different period to the building itself. A lift may be classified as 'plant and equipment'.

The useful economic lives and residual values of fixed assets should be reviewed at the end of the accounting period, and where there is a material change, the value of the asset should be depreciated over its remaining useful life. There is no need in this case to change previous years' accounts – it is merely a change in the current and future depreciation.

Residual value

Some assets will have some value at the end of their useful life. For example, a printing press may be sold when the organisation wants to upgrade to a new one. Depreciation therefore ought to be calculated on the loss in value between the original purchase price and the residual value. Assume that the printing press is purchased for £50,000 and the estimated residual value is £10,000. Depreciation needs to be calculated on £40,000 – the original purchase price less the residual value. Residual values have to be estimated when the asset is first acquired. Frequently, organisations assume that the residual value will be nil, as this is often the case with short-life assets and items such as computers.

No depreciation

The general rule in FRS 15 is that all tangible fixed assets should be depreciated. There are, however, a few exceptions to this general rule, where it is not necessary to depreciate:

◆ Freehold land is not depreciated, as it is considered to have an indefinitely long useful life. Buildings should be depreciated, because eventually they do crumble and fall. Land, however, does not waste away. Depreciation is not necessary on an asset that does not suffer wear and tear.

◆ It is not necessary to charge depreciation if the amount of the depreciation expense and the accumulated depreciation are not material. Two examples are given in FRS 15 where this may be the case:

  – The asset has a very long useful life.

  – The residual value of the asset, based on prices at the time of acquisition or revaluation, is not materially different from the amount shown in the balance sheet.

If either of these circumstances exist and depreciation is not provided, then you do need to review these assets for impairment each year (*see below for details of impairment reviews*).

Accounting policy for depreciation

The notes to the accounts need to include an accounting policy that explains the depreciation policy for the charity.

Example: Accounting policy

Aid Overseas

Capitalisation and depreciation of tangible fixed assets
All assets costing more than £1,000 are capitalised.

Freehold land is not depreciated. The cost of other tangible fixed assets is written off by equal annual instalments over their expected useful life as follows:

Freehold buildings	50 years
Leasehold property	5–10 years
Furniture, fixtures and equipment	3–10 years
Motor vehicles	4 years

Source: CC66 SORP 2000: Example Reports and Accounts

NOTES TO THE ACCOUNTS

Tangible fixed assets should be analysed in the notes to the accounts within the following categories:

- Freehold interest in land and buildings
- Leasehold and other interests in land and buildings
- Plant and machinery, including motor vehicles
- Fixtures, fittings and equipment
- Payments on account and assets in the course of construction.

These are broad categories that you may wish to adapt to suit your circumstances. For example, many charities separate computer equipment, other office equipment, and furniture and fittings. Similarly, if you have minibuses and other vehicles, you may choose to keep these separate.

The notes should summarise all material changes in the values of each class of functional fixed assets and reconcile the opening and closing balances.

Example: Tangible fixed assets note

Aid Overseas

	Freehold property	Leasehold property	Furniture, fixtures and equipment	Motor vehicles	Total
	£'000	£'000	£'000	£'000	£'000
Cost					
At 1 October 2000	1,585	3,382	2,431	379	7,777
Additions	52	205	218	13	488
Disposals	-	(18)	(32)	(88)	(138)
At 30 September 2001	1,637	3,569	2,617	304	8,127
Depreciation					
At 1 October 2000	303	2,963	1,962	291	5,519
Charge for the year	19	112	155	11	297
Disposals	6	(5)	(27)	(66)	(92)
At 30 September 2001	328	3,070	2,090	236	5,724
Net book value					
At 30 September 2001	1,309	499	527	68	2,403
At 30 September 2000	1,282	418	469	88	2,258

Source: CC66 SORP 2000: Example Reports and Accounts

IMPAIRMENT OF TANGIBLE FIXED ASSETS

When the recoverable amount of a tangible fixed asset falls below the net book value, this is termed impairment. FRS 11 requires the asset to be written down to its recoverable amount. The recoverable amount of a fixed asset is the higher of the net realisable value and the value in use.

Net realisable value is the amount the asset could be sold for in the immediate future.

Value in use is the future benefit the charity could still receive by using the asset, normally measured by future cashflows from the use of the asset. In charities, assets may not be income generating in the commercial sense, and so it is valid to consider the value of the asset continuing in service. A comparison to the option of hiring or leasing the same equipment may approximate the value of the continued use of the asset.

For example, an asset may have suffered much greater wear and tear than was anticipated, and so it is worth less than expected. It is more likely to be a major event, such as a fire, that will trigger a review. The first step is to assess the net realisable value. If this is lower than the net book value, then the value in use will have to be considered as a next step. This might involve a comparison between the overall cost of scrapping the existing asset and getting a new asset, and the overall cost of bringing the existing asset back into use and depreciating it over its remaining useful life.

An asset may have no value in use if the charity is ceasing a particular activity for which the asset was purchased. The proper basis would then be to look at the realisable value, i.e. how much the asset could be sold for. If an impairment review is carried out, the methods used to determine the value in use and net realisable value should be disclosed in the notes to the accounts.

Illustration: Realisable value

A charity has specialist climbing frames and play equipment built for an adventure playground. Unfortunately, the owner of the land used for the adventure playground repossesses the land and the charity will no longer be able to run the adventure playground. The equipment has become redundant and it is not appropriate to continue the old basis on which the equipment had been held in the accounts. In this case, they will have to consider the realisable value and change the net book value to the realisable value. The amount of the amendment is treated as additional depreciation.

An annual impairment review is required for assets that are not depreciated. However, an impairment review is also required for other assets if there is some indication that the value has fallen. As far as possible, the review should be carried out on individual assets. When this is not possible, then similar assets may be grouped together.

Examples given in the SORP of events that may trigger an impairment review include:

- physical deterioration, change or obsolescence of the asset

- social, demographic or environmental changes resulting in a reduction of beneficiaries for a charity

- changes in the law, other regulations or standards that adversely affect the activities of a charity

- management commitments to undertake a significant reorganisation

- a major loss of key employees associated with particular activities of a charity

- operating losses on activities using fixed assets primarily to generate incoming resources.

If a review indicates that the asset has been impaired, then the asset should be written down to its recoverable amount (if a decision has been made to sell the asset, it should be written down to the expected net realisable value). This loss should be treated as additional depreciation and taken to the SoFA. The revised carrying amount of the asset should be depreciated over its remaining useful economic life.

REVALUATION OF TANGIBLE FIXED ASSETS

In some cases, it will be appropriate for charities to include tangible fixed assets in the balance sheet at their current value rather than at their original cost. Though it is required under the SORP to revalue investments, it is not necessary for tangible fixed assets. If this option is chosen, there are some detailed rules that need to be followed:

- A policy of revaluation does not need to apply to all tangible fixed assets, but must be applied to all assets within the class. So, for example, if you decide that one freehold property should be revalued, then all freehold property will also need to be revalued.

- Once a policy of revaluation has been adopted, the value of the relevant fixed assets must be updated on a regular basis. Revaluation every five years is acceptable, provided the trustees obtain advice on the possibility of material changes between valuations. Where a charity has a number of revalued assets, it will be acceptable to undertake revaluations on a rolling basis over a five-year period.

- If a trustee or an employee is suitably qualified, they may undertake the valuation. However, if such a resource is not available internally, a professional will need to be used. The trustees should take the cost of this into account when considering whether to adopt such a policy.

- In the case of assets other than property, such as motor vehicles, there may be an active second-hand market for the asset, or appropriate indices may exist that allows a valuation to be obtained with reasonable certainty by an appropriate person (but not necessarily a qualified valuer). Where this method of valuation is used, the assets' values must be updated annually.

If an asset is donated and therefore brought into the balance sheet at the value of the gift, that does not constitute a policy of revaluation and the original value of the donation can be used as cost. That also applies to assets that are valued in order to initially capitalise them to follow the SORP.

Notes on revalued assets

Where a charity has revalued any class of fixed assets, the notes should disclose:

- the name and qualification of the valuer and whether they are a member of staff, a trustee or external to the charity
- the basis or bases of valuation
- where records are available, the historical cost less accumulated depreciation
- date of the previous full valuation
- if the valuation has not been updated in this reporting period, a statement by the trustees that they are not aware of any material changes since the last valuation.

Example: Note to the accounts

The majority of freehold properties were revalued as at 31 December 1998 by Weatherall Green & Smith, Chartered Surveyors on an open market basis in accordance with guidelines issued by the Royal Institute of Chartered Surveyors.

If freehold properties had not been revalued, they would have been included in the balance sheet at a cost of £58.1m and a net book value of £30.7m. The depreciation charge for the year would have been £2,755,000, compared with the actual charge of £730,000 based on the revalued amounts.

Source: The Guide Dogs for the Blind Association Report and Financial Statements 2000

Where fixed assets are revalued upwards, the difference between the original net book value and the new revalued amount is a revaluation reserve. Charitable companies need to disclose this reserve separately on the face of the balance sheet–this should be a subheading under the relevant fund in the funds section. Further information may be necessary in the notes to the accounts, and the note on the various funds of the charity will need to allocate the revaluation reserve to one or more funds of the charity.

Transitional arrangements

Some charities that have previously revalued fixed assets may now decide that the arrangements under the SORP and FRS 15 are too onerous. In that case, there are some transitional arrangements that can be adopted for the first year the SORP and FRS 15 are followed.

The charity can choose to retain the asset that has been previously revalued at the current value. That value can then be depreciated and no further revaluations will be required. If that option is chosen, the charity will need to carry out an impairment review. The accounts will also need to disclose that the transitional arrangements of FRS 15 have been adopted and that the valuation has not been updated, giving the date of the last valuation.

An alternative possibility on first application of the SORP and FRS 15 is to restate the carrying amount of tangible fixed assets to historical cost, less restated accumulated depreciation, as a change in accounting policy.

Example: Accounting policy for tangible fixed assets

Tangible fixed assets, with an historic cost of £1,000 or more including Value Added Tax, are stated in the balance sheet at cost, with the exception of freehold land and buildings, which are stated at valuation (*see below*) at the following annual rates:

Freehold land	Nil
Buildings	5%
Furniture and equipment	10%–20%
Motor vehicles	25%
Computers	33.33%

The association has applied Financial Reporting Standard (FRS) 15 Tangible Fixed Assets for the first time in the year ended 31 December 2000. The association is taking advantage of the transitional provisions within FRS 15 not to revalue the freehold land and buildings on a periodic basis in the future. Accordingly, depreciation is being charged, as noted above, to write off the valuation of the freehold land and buildings over their estimated remaining useful lives.

Source: The Guide Dogs for the Blind Association Report and Financial Statements 2000

Charities with long-held property assets should consider whether the accounts may be misleading if they do not revalue the property. The SORP requires trustees to given information if they believe that land and buildings (not held for investment purposes) included at cost less depreciation in the balance sheet have a significantly different market value. This difference should be disclosed in the notes to the accounts. If it is not practicable to quantify the difference, a written explanation will suffice.

FUNDING FOR TANGIBLE FIXED ASSETS

Where charities receive funding in the form of grants or as the result of an appeal for the purchase of fixed assets, this will represent a restricted fund. Grants should not be netted off against the cost of the asset, but the full cost of the asset should be brought onto the balance sheet. Charities do not follow SSAP 4, deferring such grants to match the income to the depreciation of the asset. Instead, the full grant should be brought in as restricted income when receivable, and the depreciation for the year will be shown as expenditure in the restricted fund. The balance at the end of a financial year that is carried forward as a restricted fund will then match the net book value of the fixed asset. This balance is available to fund future depreciation.

Illustration: Funding for tangible fixed assets

A charity is given £60,000 for the purchase and set-up of a new finance and membership computer package. During the year £54,750 has been spent on setting up the system. The remainder of the grant will be used for further training, in line with the terms of the funding, but this has not yet been spent.

It is anticipated that the computer system will be in use for 5 years and so the costs of £54,750 are to be depreciated over this time. The annual depreciation charge is therefore £54,750 divided by 5, amounting to £10,950.

In cash terms, the charity has received funding of £60,000. It has spent £54,750. The cash balance to carry forward to the next financial year to fund further training is therefore £5,250.

The expenditure on the system has been capitalised at £54,750 and depreciation is deducted to produce the net book value of £43,800 at the end of the first year. Depreciation is charged to the SoFA of £10,950 on the restricted fund.

Incoming resource	£60,000
Expenditure in year (depreciation)	£10,950
Balance on restricted fund to carry forward	£49,050

The full restricted grant has been brought in as income. The related restricted expenditure is the depreciation for the year. The balance on the restricted fund to carry forward has two components:

Net book value of the system	£43,800
Unspent grant	£5,250
	£49,050

If in the following year, the training is carried out and the unspent balance fully used, then this will be an expenditure item in the year. In the following year the restricted fund would include:

Balance brought forward	£49,050
Incoming resource	-
Expenditure in year (training)	£5,250
Expenditure in year (depreciation)	£10,950
Balance on restricted fund to carry forward	£32,850

The carried forward balance now only represents the net book value of the fixed asset after two years of depreciation.

If an asset is donated to the charity, its value on the balance sheet will match the value of the incoming resource in the SoFA. It will have been brought in at a reasonable estimate of the gross value to the charity. If the use of the gift is restricted on acquisition by the donor, then this will be treated as outlined in the example above. If there is no restriction on its use, a designated fund may be set up.

DESIGNATED FUND FOR FIXED ASSETS

There are two aspects to designating funds for fixed assets:

- setting aside funds to save for replacement assets;
- recognising the funding of existing fixed assets.

The purpose of depreciating tangible fixed assets is to fairly reflect the cost over the life of the assets. It is not a means of 'saving' for replacement assets, although the depreciation is being included in the operational costs and therefore income should be sufficient to cover this element of the cost. However, when the time comes to replace the assets it will be necessary to find cash. It may therefore be useful to set aside amounts in a designated fund, building up year by year sufficient reserves for the replacement of fixed assets when they reach the end of their useful life. This type of designated fund needs to be represented in cash.

For example, a charity requiring minibuses to transport beneficiaries may need to ensure that the vehicles can be replaced when necessary. It can budget a certain amount each year for transfer to a designated fund, building up sufficient funds for a replacement vehicle.

Designated fund to recognise funding of fixed assets

Since fixed assets are often a significant element of the balance sheet, the use of designated funds may be an appropriate tool to help readers understand the overall position of the charity. It may be misleading to readers of accounts to see the total funds, without understanding that the majority of these funds may be tied up in fixed assets.

Charities may therefore wish to set aside, as a designated fund, all or part of the current net book value of fixed assets.

Illustration: Designated fund for fixed assets

Balance Sheet at 31 March 2001

	2001		2000
	£	£	£
Tangible fixed assets		448,000	462,000
Current assets			
Debtors	24,386		35,990
Cash at bank and in hand	8,627		3,211
	33,013		39,201
Creditors: amounts falling			
due within one year	8,765		12,050
Net current assets		24,248	27,151
Net assets		472,248	489,151
Unrestricted funds			
Designated funds		448,000	462,000
General funds		10,248	14,651
Restricted funds		14,000	12,500
Total funds		472,248	489,151

The total amount of unrestricted funds held by the charity at 31 March 2001 is £458,248, which appears to be a relatively healthy position. However, £448,000 of those funds are tied up in the tangible fixed assets needed by the charity to carry out its work. This only leaves £10,248 of free reserves – clearly a rather different position. By designating the net book value of the fixed assets, the trustees are demonstrating this fact clearly for the reader of the accounts. The note to the accounts explaining the purpose of the designated fund would also include a narrative explanation to that effect.

HISTORIC AND INALIENABLE ASSETS

The fundamental principle of FRS 15 is that all assets should be capitalised on the balance sheet and depreciated. There is no exception for historical and inalienable fixed assets, as there was in the 1995 version of the SORP. Therefore, until SORP 2000 it had been common practice for charities to hold historic and inalienable assets without capitalising them.

Examples of such assets are ancient monuments, historic buildings, and collections of artistic or scientific works. Historic assets must be held as part of the charity's objects and the charity must have a policy of long retention. Inalienable and historic assets do not normally represent a store of financial resources for the charity and public access to them is often essential to demonstrate the public benefit of holding such assets.

Historic and inalienable assets

Historic assets are defined in the SORP as assets of acknowledged historic, scientific (including environmental) or artistic importance, whether of former or present times; the primary reason for retaining such assets is the direct furtherance of the charity's objects. Such assets are normally expected to be held for their lifetime and disposal should be a rare exception. In the case of a 'collection' (museums, galleries and so on), the proceeds of any individual items sold will normally be used only for their replacement, in order to maintain the collection or in accordance with the terms of trust.

An inalienable asset is defined as one which a charity is required by law to retain indefinitely for its own use/benefit and therefore cannot dispose of without external consent, whether prohibited by its governing document, the donor's wishes or in some other way. Normally the asset will belong to the charity's 'permanent endowment' where it is held on trusts which contemplate its retention and continuing use but not its disposal. However, in the case of a gift-in-kind of a 'wasting asset', such as a building, a long lease or a non-durable artefact, the terms of trust may not have provided for its maintenance in perpetuity or its replacement. In that case the endowment will be expended to the extent of the aggregate amount of its depreciation or amortisation properly provided for in the annual accounts (i.e. based on its currently anticipated useful life).

FRS 15 assumes that all assets will be capitalised, including the majority of historic and inalienable assets. Where this is the case, they should be included in a separate line in the balance sheet and can be further subdivided into classes, such as churches, collections, historic houses and artefacts. An appropriate depreciation policy will also need to be applied.

Where an inalienable or historic asset is used for administrative or fundraising purposes, such as a visitor centre or a shop, it should not be regarded as inalienable or historic. It should be capitalised within the appropriate category of tangible fixed assets for use by the charity and depreciated. An asset held as an investment should be treated in the same way as other investments, and classified appropriately. If a decision has been made to sell an asset, it should be included at its net realisable value within fixed assets or as a current asset investment.

Exemptions

The SORP provides for exemptions when it will not be necessary to value, capitalise and depreciate historic and inalienable assets. These are:

- when reliable cost information is not available and conventional valuation approaches lack sufficient reliability
- when significant costs are involved that may be onerous compared with the additional benefit derived by users of the accounts in assessing the trustees' stewardship of the assets.

The SORP explains that trustees should compare the costs and benefits of attributing a cost or value to historic or inalienable assets, taking into account valuation fees, the cost of researching past records and so on. It suggests examples of inalienable assets where a cost or valuation may not be attributable:

◆ Museum and gallery collections and other collections, including the national archives

◆ Archaeological sites, burial mounds, ruins, monuments and statues.

The exemption mainly relates to difficulties in valuing the assets. No exemption is available therefore in most situations where the charity is acquiring new assets.

◆ If an item has been recently purchased by the charity, then it will need to be included on the balance sheet, as the cost is readily available.

◆ If an item has been purchased by a third party and shortly afterwards donated to the charity, the purchase price should be taken as a reliable estimate of cost. This could also be used as a reference point for donations of similar assets.

Accounting policy and notes on historic and inalienable assets

The notes to the accounts will need to explain why the charity considers that it has assets that are historic or inalienable. Some description of the assets should be given, including the age, size and what use is made of them. Similar types of assets can be grouped together and collections can be taken as one asset. Descriptive information should be given, whether or not the assets have been capitalised. Details can only be omitted if the publication of the information would prejudice the efficient working of the charity; for example, by materially increasing the risk of theft or vandalism of the assets in question. If any inalienable and historic assets have not been capitalised or valued, a statement to this effect should be included in the notes to the accounts.

The amount spent on acquiring inalienable and historic assets during the year should be disclosed in the notes to the accounts. The accounting policy notes should include the acquisition and disposal policy for inalienable and historic assets.

Example: Accounting policy for historic and inalienable assets

The Edinburgh Educational Trust

Until 31 December 1991 neither the original cost nor improvements to freehold land and buildings were capitalised because the buildings are historic, inalienable and form part of a permanent endowment that means that these cannot be sold but must be held in perpetuity.

The original cost of the assets and the improvements thereto is not available. The users of the accounts are principally the trustees, parents of children attending the school and various donors. The trustees consider the cost of carrying out a professional valuation to include these assets at a value in the accounts to be considerable compared to the limited additional benefit derived by the users of the accounts.

Since 1 January 1992, all improvements to land and buildings costing more than £1,500 are capitalised and depreciated over 4 years. At 31 March 2001, all such assets have been fully depreciated and eliminated from these accounts.

Note to the accounts for historic and inalienable assets

The trust owns the original Georgian Mansion House built in 1757 and the Victorian Hospital designed by Hippolyte White and built in 1874, both of which are 'A' listed. These properties were originally gifted to the trust to be held in perpetuity in accordance with the trust deed and they form part of the permanent endowment funds. The original value of the assets and cost of improvements to them until 1991 has not been included in the balance sheet because, in the opinion of the trustees, the cost of professionally valuing these assets to include a value in the accounts outweighs the benefits to the users of the accounts. They are insured for £20,000,000, which is an estimate of their replacement cost.

Source: CC66 SORP 2000: Example Reports and Accounts

INFORMATION REQUIRED IN THE NOTES TO THE ACCOUNTS

The accounting policy for tangible fixed assets should include the following, where applicable:

◆ Whether each class of asset is included at cost, valuation or revaluation, and the method of valuation, where applicable.

◆ The value below which fixed assets are not capitalised.

◆ Whether inalienable and historic assets are capitalised, and if not, the reason why (for example, lack of reliable information, cost/benefit reason and so on), specifying the acquisition and disposal policies for such assets.

◆ The rates of depreciation applying to each class of fixed assets.

◆ The policy with respect to impairment reviews of fixed assets.

The notes to the accounts will need to give further information as set out in the preceding sections, depending on the sections that apply to your charity.

10 ▼ Related party transactions

This chapter looks at the requirements for transparency about transactions with people or organisations that can be said to be 'connected' to the charity or related parties. SORP 2000 has been updated to incorporate the requirements of FRS 8 and explains in some detail how the rules apply to charities. It can be helpful to break down the overall requirements into three steps:

◆ Identify related parties.
◆ Identify any transactions with them.
◆ Establish whether the transactions need to be reported.

WHAT IS A RELATED PARTY?

A related party is a person or an organisation that has a relationship with or connection to the charity. This can be a financial interest, or it may be some form of control, such as being a director or major shareholder of a company. The trustees of the charity and their close relatives will automatically be related parties to the charity. If a trustee or his or her spouse owns a business, then that business will be a related party. The list of potential related parties is long.

The senior employees of a charity will also be related parties, and will include those who have responsibility for directing or controlling the major activities or resources of the charity.

Trustees and connected persons

The trustees of a charity are always related parties. In addition, close family members of trustees are connected persons and as such are related parties to the charity. This can include friends if they influence the trustee in how they act as a trustee of the charity. The SORP refers to 'members of the same household', so this encompasses all forms of close relationships and updates old definitions of connected persons, which referred only to spouses. Close family members also includes parents, siblings and children.

In addition, there are the following categories of related parties:

◆ If a trustee or a connected person as described above is the beneficiary or potential beneficiary of a non-charitable trust, then the trustees of that trust are connected persons and as such related parties to the charity.

- The business partners of a charity trustee or a person connected to a trustee, such as a close family relative.

- A company controlled by a trustee, or where the trustee and connected persons collectively have control. Also companies where they hold more than 20% of the shares.

- If another organisation nominates a significant proportion of the trustees and makes those people available to act in their capacity as trustees, then that organisation may also be a related party. The appointed trustees would have to exert a dominant influence for the organisation appointing them to be a related party.

Hence, it can be seen that it is a wide net. A very large number of people will be related parties, although there may not be any transactions with them, and therefore nothing to report.

Shadow trustees

In company law, there is a concept of 'shadow directors'; this also applies to charities that are companies. A shadow director is someone who can issue instructions to the management or otherwise control the activities of the company, even though they have not been appointed a director of the company. Under company law, such a person will be treated in the same way as a formally appointed director.

This could arise in a charity where there are observers or co-opted members of a board or management committee. If these people participate in meetings and influence decisions, then they will be considered directors even if they are not formally appointed as such and listed at Companies House.

Similar rules apply to charities that are not companies. The SORP covers the point that a related party may exist in situations where the trustees are nominees. For example, the constitution of a charity may provide for a trustee to be nominated from another body. Shadow trustees should be treated as related parties and will include:

- any person or body with the power to appoint or remove a 'significant proportion' of the trustees of the charity

- any person or body whose consent is required for trustees to take any action

- any person or body who is entitled to give directions to the trustees.

A 'significant proportion' will be assumed to exist if it affects all or a majority of the trustees. Where the numbers involved are fewer than 50% of the trustees, then it may still be a significant proportion if they collectively have a dominant influence on the decisions of the charity. This would be the case, for example, if one body had the power to appoint or remove 7 out of a total of 15 trustees, and the other 8 trustees are appointed by 8 other bodies.

Other charities and organisations

A charity may also have connections with other charities or bodies and some of these may fall within the definition of a related party. Clearly, a sister charity providing significant funds will be a related party, as will a pension fund operated by the charity for the benefit of its employees.

If the charity controls an institution or owns more than 20% of the shares, or has more than 20% of the voting rights, then this would be a related party, as would the director of the institution.

Charities can be related parties if one charity is the trustee of the other, or if one charity can appoint a majority of the trustees of the other. Another charity will be a related party if there is 'common control'. This may occur where the trustees are all the same, or if the same person has the right to appoint all the trustees, or if they are effectively managed by the same person.

There will not be common control simply because two charities have one or two trustees in common.

RELATED PARTY TRANSACTIONS

The types of transactions that have to be considered for potential reporting as related party transactions include:

◆ payments to trustees or those connected with them

◆ any other benefits provided to trustees or persons connected with them

◆ buying, selling or leasing goods or property to or from a related party

◆ supplies of services to or from the related party, such as bookkeeping, use of premises and so on

◆ lending money, goods or property to or from the related party

◆ donations of goods, property or cash to a related party, even though these may be in furtherance of the charity's objects

◆ donations from a related party.

Transactions with trustees

There is a general provision in charity law that trustees should not benefit from their position. This means that they should receive no remuneration or benefits. This may be overridden by a specific clause in the charity's constitution allowing remuneration, which may be permitted by the Charity Commission in certain circumstances.

In general, however, trustees should receive no remuneration for their services, nor should they be paid employees of the charity, nor undertake services for which they receive payment. Trustees may be reimbursed for expenses they have incurred when acting in their capacity as a trustee, such as travel to trustee meetings. In addition, they may be paid for loss of earnings in appropriate situations. For example, a trustee giving up a whole day in their normal working week to participate in recruitment interviews for the charity would be able to claim an appropriate amount for loss of earnings. Charities may also provide childcare or an allowance for trustees if this is an expense incurred by the trustees because of attendance at meetings.

Sometimes trustees act as agents for the charity and make purchases on its behalf and are then reimbursed for this expenditure; for example, buying stationery or office equipment. This is not seen as reimbursement of expenses and does not come within the definition of a related party transaction. Likewise there is no real benefit when trustees are provided with a drink and a sandwich at a trustees' meeting.

Transactions where a third party provides the payment or benefit to a trustee are included in the definition of related party transactions. For example, if the trustees are also directors of the trading company of a charity, payments to them by the trading company would be related party transactions.

Amounts paid to close relatives or other people connected to a trustee will also count as payments to the trustee and therefore fall within the boundaries of a related party transaction. For example, the sister of a trustee may provide bookkeeping and payroll services for a fee, or a trustee who is a solicitor may involve his firm in legal advice for a fee.

In some situations, trustees may be users of the charity's services or beneficiaries of the charity. This will arise in many membership and umbrella charities and charities where there is a deliberate policy to have users on the trustee board. As long as the trustees receive any such services or benefits on the same terms as other beneficiaries, then this does not have to be reported. Any special privileges or rights should, however, be reported.

Transactions with staff

Normal transactions with staff include the contract of employment, payment of salary, pension contributions and legitimate expenses. Staff may receive other benefits, depending on the terms of employment. There are separate requirements to disclose staff costs and total emoluments (salary and benefits) in the notes to the accounts. These details do not have to be further reported as related party transactions as they are considered part of the normal business arrangements.

Exceptionally, a related party transaction would have to be reported if a member of staff were connected to a trustee, such as a close family member or business associate.

Other transactions with related parties

The purpose of the rules on reporting related party transactions is to ensure that there is transparency. As a general rule, a charity's decision to enter into a transaction should only be influenced by the charity's own interests. Charities should therefore be alert to situations where there is a potential conflict of interest. This does not make related party transactions illegal or dishonest. The transaction itself may be totally above board, but it may still be necessary to report the transaction.

For example, the brother-in-law of a trustee is the owner of a company that has supplied computers to the charity. In fact, he has allowed a significant discount on the purchase, thus saving the charity a considerable amount of money. The company has also provided a year's free hardware maintenance. This is obviously to the charity's considerable benefit, but it still needs to be reported, with enough information so that readers of the report and accounts can fully understand the transaction. It is in the charity's own interests to provide full disclosure on such matters, so that it is fully accountable.

Hence it can be seen that in the context of charities, related party transactions are not simply those that are potentially damaging to the charity, but are also transactions that may have been of benefit to the charity.

Donations and gifts in kind

Donations of goods or money to a charity from a related party do not need to be reported where the donor is not attaching conditions that change the way the charity conducts its operations. Trustees and staff supporting the charity in the same way as other supporters are not transactions that need to be reported. For example, a trustee taking part in the London Marathon to raise funds for the charity of which he or she is a trustee does not have to be reported. Similarly, buying raffles tickets or charity merchandise is usually small-scale and is not considered significant.

Intangible income such as services provided to the charity for free by trustees and other related parties also do not need to be reported. Volunteer time would also come within this category.

On the other hand, a donor who seeks to control the actions of the charity and exert influence over the way the charity conducts its activities is entering into a transaction that may need to be reported if the donor is a related party.

Transactions involving donations or gifts to related parties, whether these are to individuals or institutions, will need to be reported, even when these are in the normal course of the charity's activities.

WHEN DO WE HAVE TO REPORT RELATED PARTY TRANSACTIONS?

- Remuneration to trustees or connected persons always has to be reported as a note to the accounts. This will include contributions to a pension fund. Any amount will be considered material.
- Expenses paid to trustees, whether reimbursed to the trustee or paid via a third party.
- Purchases or sales between the charity and a trustee or anybody connected to a trustee, such as a close relative or business associate.
- Loans, guarantees, leases, property transactions, or any business arrangement between the charity and a trustee or connected persons.
- All such transactions between the charity and organisations that are related parties, e.g. charities under common control.
- When charities award grants to institutions or other charities where their trustees are either trustees or employees.

WHAT DO WE HAVE TO REPORT?

The SORP requires the following to be reported:

- The name(s) of the related parties involved in the transactions.
- A description of the relationship between the parties, including the interest of the related party or parties in the transaction.
- A description of the transaction.
- The amounts involved.
- Outstanding balances with the related parties at the balance sheet date, together with details of any provisions for doubtful debts.
- Any amounts written off as bad debts during the year.
- Any other information in connection with the transaction that is necessary for the understanding of the financial statements.

Only related party transactions that are material need to be reported in the notes to the accounts. Remember that all transactions in relation to payments to trustees are material.

Similar transactions can be grouped together and reported, or the report can be made by type of related party, unless disclosure of an individual transaction or connected transactions is necessary for an understanding of the impact of the transactions on the accounts of the charity or is a legal requirement. This is not the case for trustees' expenses and remuneration below.

Payments to trustees

◆ Where remuneration or benefits have been paid to trustees, the amounts to each named trustee must be reported. In addition, the legal authority under which the payment was made (for example, provision in the governing document of the charity, order of the court or Charity Commission) should also be given, as should the reason for such remuneration.

◆ Where the charity has made any pension arrangements for charity trustees or persons connected with them, the amount of contributions paid and the benefits accruing must be disclosed in the notes for each related party.

◆ Where neither the trustees nor any persons connected with them have received any such remuneration, this fact should be stated.

◆ The aggregate amount of trustee expenses should be reported in a note to the accounts. The note should indicate the nature of the expenses (for example, travel, subsistence, entertainment and so on) and the number of trustees involved.

◆ Where the trustees have received no such expenses, this fact should be stated.

Illustration: Remuneration of trustees

	Remuneration	Pension contributions
	£	£
A Smith	10,000	3,000
B Jones	7,000	2,000

The memorandum and articles of association allow for the payment of remuneration and pension contributions to trustees for professional services.

During the year the travel expenses of £500 were reimbursed to two trustees in respect of attendance at meetings.

TRUSTEES' ANNUAL REPORT

In addition to reporting the transactions with related parties in the notes to the accounts, the relationships between the charity and any other charities and organisations with which it cooperates in the pursuit of its charitable objectives should be explained in the trustees' annual report. This description is required whether or not there are any transactions to report in the notes to the accounts.

Illustration: Reporting related parties in trustees' annual report

Connected Charity

The ABC Charitable Trust works closely with The ABC Association Limited, which has the same objects. The ABC Association Limited performs certain aspects of the trust's work and receives a grant from the trust in order to fund this work.

CODE OF CONDUCT

It is considered good practice in charities for a code of conduct to be drawn up for trustees and senior employees that deals with matters such as potential conflicts of interest. The requirements in respect of related party transactions may assist charities in their consideration of a relevant code. It is for each charity to consider the particular circumstances of their charity, in light of the charity's objects, as to the appropriateness of particular guidance.

REGISTER OF INTERESTS

A register of interests assists in the process of identifying related parties. It is usual to ask trustees and senior staff to complete an annual declaration of their interests, whether remunerated or not. This would include all interests, whether they are organisations with whom the charity has transactions or not.

By asking for this information in advance, it aids transparency and is a way of protecting trustees by openly declaring at an early point all relationships.

A simple way to obtain the information is to ask trustees and senior staff to complete a form annually (*see below for an example*). The form should still be completed even where the trustee or staff member and their close family have no interests, with a statement to that effect. Newly appointed trustees and staff should be asked to complete a form upon appointment.

The trustees should formally review the register, at least annually, in a meeting and this should be recorded in the minutes to the meeting. This is evidence that all trustees are aware of all interests within the charity. During the year when decisions arise concerning a related party or when reviewing quotes or tenders, any person with an interest should remove themselves from the decision-making process.

Register of Interests

Date ....

Name of Trustee/Senior Member of Staff..

Employment details

Business interests

Give details of directorships, other charities where a trustee and note whether an office-holder (for example, chairman), and companies where holding is greater than 20%.

Company/Charity   Interest

Signature ....

Appendix

Accounting and auditing requirements for charities

The limits and requirements follow SORP 2000, and Accounting Regulations 2000 and 1995.

	Accounts	External scrutiny
Unincorporated charities		
Gross income over £250,000	Accruals basis following SORP	Audit by registered auditor
£100,000–£250,000	Accruals basis following SORP	Independent examination
£10,000–£100,000	Receipts and Payments Account and Statement of Assets and Liabilities	Independent examination
Less than £10,000	Receipts and Payments basis – no need to submit to Charity Commission	No external scrutiny required by law
Charitable companies		
Gross income over £250,000	Accruals basis following SORP	Audit by registered auditor
£90,000–£250,000	Accruals basis following SORP	Compilation report
Less than £90,000 required	Accruals basis following SORP	No external scrutiny

Annual accounts of charities

Part VI of the Companies Act 1993 came into force on 1 March 1996, affecting all accounting periods starting on or after that date.

After 1 March 1996 accounts must be prepared in the correct format for each financial year and submitted to the Charity Commission within ten months of the end of the financial year. The basic requirements are that larger charities must prepare a Statement of Financial Activities (SoFA) and a balance sheet. The accounting regulations also specify explanatory notes, which must accompany accounts, and the categories in which items should be shown in the main statements. There are some exceptions from these requirements for smaller unincorporated charities.

Charities not exceeding the £250,000 threshold

The SORP recommends that charities describe expenditure by activity and then give details of the breakdown into the normal expense-type headings in the notes to the accounts. However, under the accounting regulations, charities with gross income up to £250,000 may simplify the description of their expenditure in the SoFA. This means that they may use the normal expense-type headings they may have used in their old income and expenditure account; for example, salaries, rent, rates, light, heat and so on. This means that the SoFA for many smaller charities will not be very different to the old income and expenditure account.

Charities not exceeding the £100,000 threshold

Unincorporated charities with a gross income of not more than £100,000 may choose to prepare a simpler form of accounts. These should comprise a receipts and payments account and be accompanied by a statement of assets and liabilities. This will be instead of the SoFA and balance sheet. There is no prescribed format set out in the regulations, but the Charity Commission have produced practical guidance with example accounts in their guide CC64 Receipts and Payments Accounts Pack 2001. The Charity Commission will accept the completion of their standard form instead of a separate set of accounts; this is laid out in such a way as to collect all the necessary information.

These smaller charities may choose to prepare accounts under the accruals basis if they so wish, but if they do, then they must comply with the requirements of the accounting regulations and follow the recommendations of the SORP. Accruals accounts must consist of a SoFA and a balance sheet. The Charity Commission provide guidance to these charities in their publication CC65 Accruals Accounts Pack.

Charities not exceeding the £10,000 threshold

Even smaller charities with neither gross income nor total expenditure exceeding £10,000 have to prepare accounts, but do not have to submit them to the Charity Commission unless requested to do so. In the case of unincorporated charities, these may be on the receipts and payments basis or accruals basis.

Exempt charities

These are certain categories of charities that are exempt from registration with the Charity Commission and the sections of the act relating to accounts and audit. In practice these charitable bodies are usually already subject to specific provisions relating to their accounts and audit under other regulatory bodies. Exempt charities are listed in Schedule 2 to the act.

The accounts of these charities should follow the SORP, unless a more specific SORP applies, such as with universities and housing associations.

Excepted charities

These are certain categories of charities that do not have to register with the Charity Commission, although they may register if they wish. If they do register, then they must send in their annual report and accounts to the Charity Commission. However, if they are not registered, then they do not need to submit reports and accounts. The trustees still have a statutory duty to prepare annual accounts and they have to comply with other requirements, such as sending their accounts to a member of the public if requested to do so.

Charitable companies

The relevant sections of the *Charities Act 1993* (sections 41 – 44) and Accounting Regulations 3 to 9 concerning the form and content of accounts do not apply to charitable companies. They are required to prepare accounts in the form prescribed by the Companies Acts and these accounts must show a true and fair view. In order to comply with the requirement to show a true and fair view, charitable companies will be expected to comply with the SORP. In practice, therefore, the format of their accounts should be very similar to that of unincorporated charities, although certain charitable companies may need to prepare a summary income and expenditure account as well as a SoFA. It does mean that charitable companies cannot opt for the receipts and payments basis; all accounts of companies must be prepared under the accruals basis and must be submitted to Companies House within ten months of the financial year-end. (Note: There are penalties for the late submission of accounts to Companies House, starting at £100 for accounts up to 3 months late, and rising to £250 for accounts filed 3 to 6 months late, £500 for accounts filed 6 to 12 months late, and £1,000 for accounts filed more than 12 months late.)

Charity Commission filing

Apart from the small charities up to the £10,000 threshold, all registered charities must submit their annual report and accounts within ten months of the financial year-end to the Charity Commission, including charitable companies. In practice, the Charity Commission will be asking charities to submit their report and accounts with the completed annual return for the year. The information required on the return will include extracts from the accounts, so it will in any case be easier to complete these all at the same time. Note that all charities will have to complete the annual return, including small charities.

Charity annual reports and accounts are available for public inspection at the Charity Commission offices.

In addition, members of the public may request a copy of the latest annual accounts of the charity and the charity must send them within two months. The charity may charge a reasonable fee for doing so, to cover photocopying and postage costs, for example.

Audit requirements

Prior to the Charities Act 1993, unincorporated charities were not required by statute to have an audit. The trust deed or constitution may have set out an audit requirement, or it may have been a condition of certain funders. Section 43 of the Charities Act 1993 requires larger charities to have an audit for financial years commencing on or after 1 March 1996. This part of the Charities Act 1993 does not apply to companies, as the audit regime for companies is already set out in the Companies Acts.

Larger charities are those with gross income or total expenditure exceeding £250,000; they must be audited by a registered auditor. A registered auditor is an auditor who is qualified to undertake audits of companies and is regulated in his or her work. Firms of accountants are usually registered auditors. If a large charity's gross income and total expenditure drops below the threshold of £250,000, it must continue to have a professional audit for a further two years.

Independent examination

Smaller charities, i.e. those with gross income and total expenditure not exceeding £250,000, may have an 'independent examination' instead of an audit. This is a new type of external examination brought in by the Charities Act 1993. It may be undertaken by anyone with some experience of accounting; they do not have to be a qualified accountant or auditor. Detailed guidance on independent examinations has been issued by the Charity Commission. Charities in this category may choose to have an audit, if the trustees think it is wise or if they have relatively complex affairs. It will be necessary to have an audit if the constitution requires it or if it is required by funders.

Very small charities, i.e. those with gross income and total expenditure not exceeding £10,000, do not need to have a statutory audit or an independent examination, but they also must check their constitution and their funders' requirements.

Smaller and very small charities may need to contact the Charity Commission for advice on how the constitution may be amended so that they can take advantage of the reliefs from audit.

Audit of charitable companies

Larger charitable companies are required to have an audit by a registered auditor. Charitable companies with gross income below £250,000 and net assets of less than £1.4 million may opt to have a compilation report instead of an audit. (For non-charitable companies the threshold is £350,000 turnover and there is no requirement for a compilation report.)

Companies with a gross income up to £90,000 and a balance sheet total less than £1.4 million are not required to have an audit or a compilation report.

Additional rules

There are some extra rules that companies must follow:

◆ All companies that are a subsidiary or have a subsidiary must have a full audit, regardless of turnover.

- Small groups are exempt from audit as long as they are not a public company, banking or insurance company or an authorised person under the Financial Services Act 1986. However, to qualify, the group turnover has to be below the £250,000 threshold.

- All companies must prepare full accruals accounts and submit accounts to Companies House.

- 10% of the membership can request that an audit be performed, even if the company otherwise qualifies for the exemption.

There is no rule about the audit requirement continuing as there is for unincorporated charities; the test is applied to the current year only.

Compilation report

A compilation report is independent confirmation that the accounts have been properly prepared from the accounting records. It does not seek to confirm that the accounting records themselves are complete and accurate. An accountant will often prepare the accounts as well, although they could just review the accounts and compare them with the underlying records. The accountant ensures that the accounts are presented properly and disclose all the information required under the Companies Acts. He or she then reports under an 'Accountant's Report', confirming that the accounts have been properly prepared.

Further information

Legislation

Charities Act 1993

The Charities (Accounts and Reports) Regulations 2000 (SI 2000 No. 2868)

The Charities (Accounts and Reports) Regulations 1995

Charity Accounts and Reports: Core Guide (ISBN 011 34 1156 1) This contains the regulations and relevant extracts from the legislation.

Law Reform (Miscellaneous Provisions) (Scotland) Act 1990

Charities Act (Northern Ireland) 1964

Charities (Northern Ireland) Order 1987

The Trustee Act 2000

All can be ordered from The Stationery Office website (www.the-stationery-office.co.uk) or by telephoning customer services on 0870 600 5522.

Charity Commission

Accounting and Reporting by Charities: Statement of Recommended Practice (SORP 2000)

CC8 Internal Financial Controls for Charities

CC11 Payment of Charity Trustees

CC19 Charities Reserves

CC20 Charities and Fund-Raising

CC23 Exempt Charities

CC24 Users on Board: Beneficiaries who become Trustees

CC35 Charities and Trading

CC37 Charities and Contracts

CC38 Expenditure and Replacement of Permanent Endowment

CC49 Charities and Insurance

CC60 The Hallmarks of Well-Run Charity

CC61 Charity Accounts 2001: the framework

CC62 Charities SORP 2000: what has changed?

CC63 Independent Examination of Charities 2001: Directions and Guidance Notes

CC64 Receipts and Payments Accounts Pack 2001

CC65 Accruals Accounts Pack

CC66 SORP 2000 Example Reports and Accounts

Useful Guidelines: Charities and Social Investment
(www.charitycommission.gov.uk/supportingcharities/pdfs/casi.pdf)

Charities and Risk Management
(www.charitycommission.gov.uk/supportingcharities/charrisk.asp)

Accounts Helpline 0870 333 0123

All available via the Charity's Commission's website (www.charitycommission.gov.uk)
or their publications orderline (01823 345427).

Books available from the Directory of Social Change

The Charity Treasurer's Handbook, Gareth G Morgan, 1st edition 2002
This is an invaluable starter guide for trustees and other charity workers with no formal accounting knowledge, as well as those who have some financial knowledge but are new to the voluntary sector. Includes information on financial management, book-keeping principles, audit and independent examination, and much more. ISBN 1 900360 89 6

The Charity Trustee's Handbook, Mike Eastwood, 1st edition 2001
This book offers guidance on the responsibilities of management committees and offers advice on planning the work of the organisation, getting funding, and managing staff and resources. ISBN 1 900360 88 8

Financial Stewardship of Charities, Adrian Poffley, 1st edition 2002
This book looks at an adaptive model of managing finances and managing organisations. Helpful sections on developing financial strategy and policies on reserves, as well as a handbook for senior finance managers and treasurers. ISBN 1 903991 17 X

A Practical Guide to Financial Management, Kate Sayer, 2nd edition 2002
This covers financial planning, budgeting, financial controls, investing, trading by charities, computerising your accounts and tax-effective giving. ISBN 1 903991 29 3

A Practical Guide to VAT, Kate Sayer, 2nd edition 2001
Specifically written for charities, this provides an introduction to VAT, and introduces the basic principles and categories of VAT. It then goes on to cover more complex areas such as VAT recovery, partial exemption, international aspects of VAT, and VAT planning. ISBN 1 900360 62 4

The Voluntary Sector Legal Handbook, Sandy Adirondack and James Sinclair Taylor, 2nd edition 2001

This covers employment law, constitutional issues and many other areas, including investment powers. ISBN 1 900360 72 1

To order any of these books, please contact:

DSC Books
Tel: 020 7209 5151; Fax 020 7391 4804
E-mail: books@dsc.org.uk; website: www.dsc.org.uk

Other books

The Governance and Management of Charities, Andrew Hind
This looks in detail at the role of trustees and senior management in a charity and how the two should interface. It also covers strategic planning and financial policies. ISBN 0 9525801 0 1

Not Just for a Rainy Day?, Shirley Gillingham and John Tame
This is a detailed guide for trustees and charity managers on how to approach the issue of reserves, planning for reserves and assessing the right level of reserves. Published by NCVO. ISBN 0 7199 1516 3

Financial Management in the Voluntary Sector, Paul Palmer and Adrian Randall
This describes the main applications of accounting and finance as they apply to the role of a financial manager. Published by Routledge. ISBN 0 415 22160 9

Funding our future II: Understanding and Allocating Costs, Martin Brookes, 2nd edition 2001
This is a report as well as a guide on the issue of core costs and how voluntary organisations can allocate such costs so that they are included in funding bids. Published by ACEVO and available via their website (www.acevo.org.uk). ISBN 1 900685 10 8

Other sources of information

Sayer Vincent website – (www.sayervincent.co.uk)

Information for charities and not-for-profit organisations, with updates and links to other relevant websites.

Directory of Social Change

The Directory of Social Change runs the largest programme of training courses, seminars and conferences in the UK voluntary sector. For full details, phone for a copy of the latest Training Guide.

DSC Courses and conferences
Tel: 020 7209 4949 (London); 0151 708 0117 (Liverpool)
E-mail: training@dsc.org.uk; website: www.dsc.org.uk

Charity Finance

A magazine published 10 times a year and available by subscription. Contains articles and updates, as well as comparative information on investment performance and banking. (www.charityfinance.co.uk)

EIRIS

The Ethical Investment Research Service provides independent research into corporate behaviour for those who wish to make judgements about the investments they choose on ethical grounds. (www.eiris.org)

The WM Company

The UK's largest performance measurement company for investments. It provides a benchmarking service for segregated charity funds. Performance of common investment funds regularly reproduced in Charity Finance magazine. Factsheet available from WM on 020 7547 7966.

Association of Charity Independent Examiners (ACIE)

The association provides support, training, and a professional qualification for anyone acting (or wishing to act) as an independent examiner of charity accounts. ACIE is itself a charity, seeking to promote the greater effectiveness of other charities by supporting independent examiners.

36 Acomb Wood Drive, York YO24 2XN
Tel: 01904 788885; Fax: 01904 339117
E-mail: info@acie.org.uk; Website: www.acie.org.uk

Index

accountants' reports/compilation reports 9, 147

accounting policies, details of 29

accruals basis 9, 20

administration see management and administration costs

advertising costs 20, 100, 101

agent's fees, cost of 20, 100

annual reports see trustees' annual reports

appeals, fundraising 16–i17

    costs 92

    and reserves policies 48

    for specific purposes 22, 80, 85, 128

archaeological sites 132

assets 9

    fixed 10, see also tangible fixed assets

    inalienable 11; see historic and inalienable assets

    net book value 12, 119

    net realisable value 12

    residual value 12, 121, 122

auctions 19

auditors 12, 38

audits

    costs 21, 104

    requirements 15, 145–147

    of summarised financial statements 38

balance sheets 9, 24, 25

bank interest 17

Barnardo's 63

benchmarking

    and investment policies 59

    and reserves policies 48

British Heart Foundation 62

budgeting for costs 93

buildings see historic and inalienable assets; premises; property; tangible fixed assets

Camberwick Community Hall 50–51

capital/capital funds 9, 13, 59, 68, 80, 81

capitalisation (of assets) 9, 29, 117, 118

cash deposit accounts 58, 59, 62, 68

cashflow

    forecasts 69

    and implications of restricted funds 89–90

    statements 26, 28

    and timing 54

charitable expenditure see under expenditure

charitable trading 84

Charities (Accounts and Reports) Regulations 2000 ('the regulations') 40

Charities Act 1993 15, 145, 146

Charity Commission 15, 30, 67, 77, 91, 136

    audit requirements 143–145

    example reports and accounts 29, 45, 46, 61, 62, 72, 76, 78, 107–108, 122, 123, 133

    guidance on independent examinations 146

    guidance on investments 59, 60

    guidance on reserves 47

    investigations 47, 58, 80, 89

charity shops 19, 100

Christmas card sales 20, 101

City Parochial Foundation 79

'common control', charities under 136, 139

Common Deposit Funds 59

Common Investment Funds 59, 66, 68

communication costs 21

Companies Acts 15, 25, 26, 30, 64, 143, 145, 147

compilation reports *see* accountants' reports

computers 121, 123, 128 see *also* software systems

'conflicts of interest' 138

contracts

    costs of monitoring and reporting progress 20

    income from 84–85

    negotiation costs 20, 101

core costs: and funding 83, 92, 93, 94

costs

    and accounting policies 106–107, 116

    of activities in furtherance of charity's objects 100, 103

    allocating 29, 94, 100–116

    analysis of 107–108

    of appeals 92

    and budgeting 93

    core 83, 92, 93, 94

    direct and indirect 104–106

    and funding applications 93

    of generating funds 10, 20–21, 100–102

    of grantmaking 102

    management and administration 12, 21, 100, 102, 104

    support 13, 20, 21, 101, 102, 103, 110

    see also expenditure

custodian trustees 36

deferred income 85–86

depreciation (of fixed assets) 18, 21, 29, 86, 87, 118–121, 122, 123

derivatives 59

designated funds 10, 23, 47, 50, 73, 86, 91

for fixed assets 129–130

Diana, Princess of Wales Memorial Fund 73, 79

direct mail, cost of 20, 100

discontinued activities 25, 26

donations 17, 22

    from related parties 138

    as income stream 51, 52, 53

'duty of care' 57

Edinburgh Educational Trust 13

EIRIS 60, 63, 151

endowment funds 10, 50

    expendable 10, 23, 80, 81–82

    new 16, 17, 25, 81

    permanent 12, 22, 59, 80–81

    transferring 24, 90–91

equipment

    as gifts in kind 18

    see tangible fixed assets

ethical investments 57, 60, 62–63

expenditure

    category headings on SoFA 20, 100

    charitable 9, 21–22, 100, 102–104

    reviewing patterns 54–55

    total 13

    see also costs

expenses, reimbursement of 137, 139, 140

Financial Reporting Standards 10, 15, 25, 26, 77, 117, 118, 122

financial statements 10

    format and contents 16

    summarised 37–38

fixed assets 10

    investments 68

    see tangible fixed assets

fixtures and fittings *see* tangible fixed assets

foreign currency transactions 29

freehold buildings: and depreciation 121, 122, 123

freehold land 122, 127

fund accounting 22–23 see restricted funds; unrestricted funds

funding applications: and cost allocations 93

fundraising appeals see appeals, fundraising

fundraising costs 20–21, 92, 100–101

funds

    analysis of existing 50–51

    brought and carried forward 24

    costs of generating 10, 20–21, 100–102

    general 10, 23

    reviewing future 51–53 see designated funds; endowment funds; reserves; restricted funds; unrestricted funds

gallery collections 132

general funds 10, 23

gifts in kind 16, 18–19, 29, 32, 87

    from related parties 138

Gillingham, Shirley and Tame, John: Not Just for a Rainy Day? 49

goods

    donated for charity's own use 18

    donated for distribution 19

    donated for resale 19

    from related parties 138

    sales of 20, 100–101

governing documents 11, 58, 140

grants and grantmaking 21, 71

    accounting treatments 77–79

    administrative costs 21, 102

    analysis in notes to the accounts 74–77, 78–79

    analysis in separate publications 76–77

    award letters 77, 79

    for core funding 83

    disclosure on SoFA 71

    material to charities 71

    policies explained in trustees' annual reports 72–73

    and reserves policies 51, 55, 73

    as restricted funds 22, 80, 83, 84, 85, 86, 93, 128

    reviewing 79

    for tangible fixed assets 128–129

    and timeframes 17

gross income 11

Guide Dogs for the Blind Association Report & Financial Statements 67, 126, 127

Hind, Andrew 48

historic and inalienable assets 11, 118, 130–132

impairment 11, 124–125

inalienable assets 11, 131; see historic and inalienable assets

income (see incoming resources)

    analysing existing 50–51

    deferred 85–86

gross 11

    intangible 19–20, 32

    reviewing future 51–53

    voluntary 14, 17

income and expenditure accounts 11, 16, 23, 25–26, 27

incoming resources 11, 16–17

independent examinations 11, 146, 151

Industrial and Provident Societies 15

insolvency 89

intangible income 16, 19–20, 29, 32, 138

investment management 58, 61, 62, 68, 69
 fees 21, 101

investment policies (*see also* investments)
 and assessment of available funds
 68–69
 ethical 57, 60, 62–63
 monitoring by benchmarking 59
 programme-related 60–61
 and reserves policies 57, 69
 reviewing 57
 and risk 57, 58
 socially-responsible 60
 statement in trustees' annual reports
 57, 59, 61
 total return approach 59, 61, 62, 68,
 82

investment properties 66, 70

investments 17
 accounting for 63–65, 69–70
 information required in notes to the
 accounts 65–68
 keeping registers of 69–70
 material 67
 realised and unrealised gains and
 losses 63–65
 revaluations of 24, 25, 63, 68
 trustees' management of 57, 58
 types 57, 58–59
 see investment policies

Islington Children's Playgroups 84, 85

land 118, 123
 freehold 122, 127
 investment in 58

Law Reform (Miscellaneous Provisions)
 (Scotland) Act 1990 26

leasehold property 29, 118, 123

and depreciation 121, 122, 123

legacies 17, 80, 81

legal costs 104, 118

liabilities 12, 29

lifts: and depreciation 121

management and administration costs 12,
 21, 100, 102, 104

marathons 53

'material' 12

membership subscriptions 51

monuments 132

motor vehicles *see* vehicles

museum collections 132

National Association of Victim Support
 Schemes 28

net book value 12, 119–120, 123, 126

'net incoming resources available for
charitable application' 101, 102

net realisable value 12, 124

Northern Ireland charities 15, 16

notes to the accounts 28–29, 106–107

office running costs *see* support costs

overhead expenses 92, 93

overseas development charities 19

overseas fundraising events 53

Oxfam 106

Oxford, Bishop of: v. Church Commissioners
 (court case) 60

payroll services 19

pensions 29, 140

permanent endowment funds *see under*
 endowment funds

plant and machinery *see* tangible fixed
 assets

premises
    costs 22, 104, 105
    use of as intangible income 19–20
    see also property
profit 16
profit and loss accounts 16; see income and
    expenditure accounts
programme-related investments 60–61
projects
    cost of management 21
    grants towards 22
promotion see publicity costs
property
    buying costs 118
    depreciation 121, 122, 123
    improvements to 118
    for investment 66, 70
    leasehold 29, 118, 121, 122, 123
    and reserves policies 50–51
    revaluations 24, 127
    see also premises
publicity costs 20, 100, 101

raffles 19, 138
realised gains and losses 63–65, 69
receipts and payments accounts 12
register of interests 141–142
related parties 134–136
    charities 136
    donations and gifts in kind 138
    identifying 141–142
    transactions 136–139
rent 19–20, 22, 105
reports
    accountants' or compilation 9, 147
    see trustees' annual reports
reserves 47

approaches to developing policies
    (Hind) 48–49
and assessing funds available for
    investment 69
benefits of developing policies 47,
    48–49
and designated funds 47
drawing policies up 56
and grantmaking 51, 55, 73
and investment policies 57, 69
reasons for holding 49
and risk identification 49, 51, 55
steps in developing policies 49–55
residual value 12, 121, 122
resources
    expended see expenditure
    incoming 11, 16–17
restricted funds 13, 22, 23, 50, 80
    in deficit 87
    identifying assets in 91–92
    identifying costs to 92–94
    listing in notes to the accounts 91
    managing cashflow implications 89–90
    for purchase of fixed assets 86
    recording and monitoring 94–99
    and reviewing future income streams
    53
    transferring funds from unrestricted
    funds 87, 90, 99
    transferring to unrestricted funds 88,
    91
    and unrestricted funds in deficit 87–89
    see also endowment funds; restricted
    income funds
restricted income funds 23, 80, 82–83, 85
    contractual income 84–85
    deferred income 85–86

gifts of fixed assets 18, 87

grants 22, 80, 83, 84, 85, 86, 93

and overhead expenses 92, 93

recognising 83–84, 85

revaluations 24, 29, 125–127

risk assessments 40

identifying risks 40–41

prioritising risks 41–43

taking appropriate action 44

see also investments; reserves

risk registers 45

risk reviews 45, 46

risk statements (in trustees' annual reports) 31, 45–46

Rosanna Grant Trust 61, 72, 76, 78, 108

salaries 21, 22, 55, 104, 105, 110, 111–115

Save the Children 56

scholarships see grants and grantmaking

school fees 17

Scottish charities 13, 15, 16, 26

services

and contractual income 84

donation of 19

sales of 20

shadow trustees 135

socially responsible investments 60

SoFA see Statement of Financial Activities

software systems, accounting 94, 105

SORP (Statement of Recommended Practice)/SORP 2000 15, 16, 40, 47, 57, 63, 64, 130

staff

register of interests 141–142

and related party transactions 137

salaries 21, 22, 55, 104, 105, 110, 111–115

secondments 19

time 20, 100, 105

statement of assets and liabilities 13

Statement of Financial Activities (SoFA) 13, 16, 23–24, 25, 27, 68, 71, 81, 82, 97–99, 143

preparing 104–107

Statement of Recommended Practice see SORP

statues 132

stock 13, 29

stocks, government 59

subscriptions, membership 51

subsidiary companies 17, 21, 101

summarised financial statements 37–38

support costs 13, 20, 21, 101, 102, 103, 110

Tame, John see Gillingham, Shirley

tangible fixed assets 13, 117

capitalisation limit 117

cost of 118

depreciation of 18, 21, 29, 86, 118–121, 122, 123

designating funds for 129–130

funding for 50, 86, 128–129

as gifts in kind 18, 87

historic and inalienable assets 130–133

impairment of 124–125

information required in notes to the accounts 123, 133

mixed use of 118

residual value 121, 122

revaluation of 125–127

treatment on balance sheet 118

'useful life' 121, 122

trading, charitable 84

trading companies 137

see also subsidiary companies
transfers between funds 24, 87, 88, 90–91, 99
transparency 73, 109, 138, 141
Trustee Act 2000 58, 60, 61
trustees
    code of conduct 141
    and investments 57, 58, 59
    pension arrangements 140
    register of interests 141–142
    as related parties 134–135
    and related party transactions 136–138, 139
    remuneration or benefits 136–137, 139, 140
    shadow 135
    and summarised financial statements 37–38
trustees' annual reports 30
    description of charity's work and achievements 32–36
    grantmaking policy statements 72–73, 74–76
    information on funds held as custodian trustee 36
    investment policy statements 57, 59, 61
    language and use of terms 31
    legal and administrative details 30–31
    references to donated goods 19
    reporting of transactions 140–141
    requirements 30, 32
    reserves policy statement 47, 56
    risk statements 31, 45–46; see risk assessments
trustees' meetings, cost of 21

unit trusts 59, 66
unrealised gains and losses 25, 63–65, 69, 70
unrestricted funds 14, 23, 24
    and allocation of costs 93
    deferred income 85–86
    in deficit 87–89
    transferring to restricted funds 87, 90, 99 see also reserves
'useful life' 118, 119, 121, 122

'value in use' 124
vehicles
    and depreciation 121, 122, 123
    designating funds for 129
    valuing 18, 126
voluntary income 14, 17
volunteer time 20

Waste Watch 32–36
Wellcome Trust 75
WM Company 59, 151